Front cover photo:;- S

How often is it in life, that we fail to understand that which someone so dearly wanted to share with us?

For Sarah
just some of
the secrets
Richard

Part One

Reflections on a tai chi journey

By Richard J Small

My undying thanks to those great teachers who have shared their own learning with me.

Published by www.goodnessmepublishing.co.uk

Note well.

Any exercises or advice within in this book should be examined while engaging your own common sense. The book is about reflections on a personal journey; the sort of journey in which we all make decisions for ourselves.

Sometimes we make mistakes.

Take responsibility for your own actions, it's part of your own journey.
In this book you will find some repeated messages. To remove them would be to rob you of timely reminders - so I haven't!

'Practising tai chi or aikido requires you to find a good teacher who can guide you.'

'Through patience will come the answer'

Tai Chi - This book gives insights into this wonderful and enlightening art through the medium of story and simple advice.

The Chinese often passed down their knowledge in story form, sometimes poetical, usually in code. This may have been for many reasons ... mainly secrecy - only those who were taught would understand the meaning ... it was a way of assisting memory. It engendered feelings as opposed to technical thought.

There are many analogies and stories within this book, which it is hoped will shine a light on some of the secrets hiding in the darkness of our own making.

My words may seem empty .... though the discovery behind them for me, has been awesome. The more we find out, the more we realise there is still much to discover.

Many times the finest adjustment will manifest itself in the biggest change. There is an awareness of change being the constant. The principles are unchanging and it is **we** that must change. Knowing this, somehow inhibits my writing .... for I know that tomorrow may bring yet another change. The truth for each of us is as we see it at the time, but the essential benefits of our art will remain a constant truth.

'The truth of our art is how we perceive it on the day, this day, this moment.'

Even when you think you have arrived and that you know everything ... remind yourself that you do not, and keep looking, for nothing is ever as it seems.

Become calm, become quieter and all that was always known to you will be revealed in a new light, but when it is, you will never explain it, for such words do not exist in the thinking world. The Gods do not allow it.

"Principles remain a constant, it is our understanding that changes."

'What ever part of Tai Chi you lay your hand on, know that you have as much chance as anyone else to find the rest of it'

Dedication:-

Dedicated to the honest and humble reader willing to diligently search this book for something of value and not just complain about the mistooks.

Contents.

1. Tai Chi – a simplistic view.

What exactly is tai chi? It seems that the longer you practise and the more you study, the harder it is to explain. For the persistent student this doesn't matter, because they focus on a journey and not a destination. At one level, tai chi chuan is an awesome martial art, at another, a sequence of simple, soft flowing movements that relax and energise. There is a philosophy behind it all - one which even provides an opposite view to my earlier words of soft, easy and relaxed.
Tai chi is a long but interesting journey in which you can discover much about yourself and life and which you would otherwise never know. There is an excitement to the discoveries you make, no matter that thousands before you also made them.

Chinese teachings often use the magic of story to convey beautiful movements that beneficially affect the body's nervous system. Calm breath, quiet mind, and evocative and inspiring moves like 'carry tiger to the mountain', 'white crane spreads wings', 'jade lady works at shuttles', 'wave hands like clouds'. (Each conveys a feeling via our imagination and is linked to the physical movement. But that is not all. No, there is much more for you to find for yourself. The fascination with story invokes the spirit and purifies intention, which in turn invites the body to take the same journey. The mind leads the body not by command but by invitation. To the practitioner it seems as though the body is moving of its own accord. Of course it isn't but the muscle feed back is absent. It is alchemy!
The body movement is only **apparently** occurring of its own accord but it is merely joining with the spirit and intention, much like a good friend wants to travel with you on a journey.

The ability to shift consciousness should never be underrated.

Most if not all teachers are still developing their art because they have felt tangible benefits to body and mind. They know how good the art is and would like nothing more than others to know it too. They will all have your interest at heart. The teacher must also learn to overcome the sadness of not finding students who appreciate the value of their teaching. Those deaf or blind to wisdom will always be difficult to reach but it is still worth trying.
Regardless of age or ability there are health benefits to be had. More and more it has been possible for technical researchers to identify the value of tai chi in terms of muscle tone, immune system, brain chemistry and nervous system.

Tai chi has a value far beyond your imagination

It's not about being better than others
but gaining victory over oneself.

2. On Learning.

Tai Chi is full of paradox, yin and yang seem to make it so, but there is more to the understanding and of that, mere words cannot suffice.

Try to learn from the experience of your own practice. Try not to return to your teacher with a fault that they have already corrected. Try to constantly change what you do, for progress creates a never ending pathway into a trackless desert.

Develop and encourage your own free thinking and remember, tai chi is there to improve your quality of life, not create more problems. In practise, never accept a problem.

Consistent and correct practise will create the mind-body pathways that allow an almost spiritual natural power to be produced .... There is only one path to this place !

'Don't let your yesterday spoil today.'

'It is you that must walk to the temple door,
to know and value how far it was.'

Morning practise in Queenstown NZ

3. Tai Chi and Holistic Living.

"Ah, so you're interested in holistic living, I hear. Have you ever thought about Tai Chi?"
'Oh, that's that new tea drink isn't it? .... no, wait a minute, I know, don't tell me...it's that thing that old people do slowly in parks in China.'
Of course there will be many views on what tai chi really is. Tai chi teachers will surely tell you, the destination is not so important, (for you may never arrive) but that every moment on the journey is to be treasured.

'It is better to consider the journey itself as your destination.'

The Oxford English dictionary states;
Tai Chi Ch'uan; The ultimate source and limit of reality from which springs yin and yang and all of creation.

Now surely you can't get much more holistic than that? Just because tai chi is seen as an old people thing it does not mean that it should be practised as though you were an old person. You can be part of something much greater.
The Chinese have been successfully evolving Chi Kung for thousands of years and based on ancient martial arts, their Tai Chi for centuries. Their development of acupressure, acupuncture and discovery of meridian lines and points throughout the body are now well known and accepted in the West. In some ways the Chinese culture allowed them answers long before the West had even considered the questions, for example, long before western science discovered 'black holes' in space, the Chinese knew they existed. Why? Because of their yin/yang philosophy, both must exist if anything is to exist, (you cannot have only one

side to a sheet of paper can you?) therefore, if there was a bright Sun in the sky, somewhere there must be a dark Sun.

Tai chi touches on many of these elements. Though originating from truly formidable martial arts it is rarely practised so today but instead is used as an exercise to promote health and longevity. Did I hear someone ask, 'What use is longevity without health?' Quite right, we wish to live long but enjoy good health in the process, and this is the purpose of tai chi. As we age, time inexorably seeks to shrink our muscles and close our joints; the tai chi practitioner fights back with exercises that allow us to grow and open our bodies as well as develop spirit. Tai chi has become not so much self defence, but health defence.

As in other spiritually aligned arts such as Yoga, certain points of the body take on a magnified significance; the crown of the head, *bai hui*, celestial gate, place of a hundred meetings, it's the connection point to the heavens from which we are suspended. The ball of the foot, *yong chuan*, connects us to the earth. All that lies between these two points should be harmonious and free.

'Heaven, Earth and you – in harmony, three together.'

The style or form you practice matters little compared to earnestly following the principles. When you read of the principles you may or may not make sense of them, only by feeling will the understanding arrive – and then tomorrow yet a new understanding ….. and then another.

Regardless whether practised for martial or health purpose, tai chi aids the flow of energy through the entire body; this is central to the benefits. Sometimes the process is uncomfortable. Free flowing and conscious movements can unravel old tensions and hidden injuries from the past,

through muscles and joints that are out of tune with nature, fettered by the chains of some past misguided protection.
So, engage your whole body, when one thing moves, all moves, the flow of energy, the unification of mind body and spirit in a conscious way, this is tai chi. *(It is also aikido.)*
'Ah yes, but what can that do for me?'
Well, Chi Kung practitioners have been shown to improve their T cell (white blood cell) count by up to 40%. The movement of the legs in tai chi (and chi kung) promotes blood flow to the heart and additionally stimulates the lymphatic system. Tai chi can boost your immune system.
Tai chi movements also stimulate your parasympathetic nervous system, (the system that keeps you calm and alive during sleep - *this is the author's simplistic version of understanding*).

'Tai chi has no enemies, no critics.'

Scientific research has recently heaped confirmation on the health benefits to add to that which any practitioner feels on a personal level. Tai chi is a healing exercise that develops physiological function without reliance on drugs, medicine or surgery. (That is not to say that some of these medical interventions may not be necessary in serious cases). So, tai chi is a healing exercise – but practise it well and you may not get to the stage where you require that medical intervention!
'Okay, so apart from better balance, greater mobility, better co-ordination and improved immune system, what has tai chi got in it for me?'
Well, once you've learned a few moves and taken on board the principles, tai chi is cost free and available any time of day or night, anywhere in the world – because it's yours to keep. Surely there can be no doubt of its holistic nature, in effect you become your own therapist. Your whole body is treated by toning the nervous system and circulation of the blood. It improves the body's ability to absorb and transport nutrients,

so increasing immunity. Tai chi is positive in all aspects, developing confidence and power. Tai chi is natural, with no negative side effects when followed correctly. So you see, tai chi is not just old people slowly waving arms in the park, they have been there from their youth.

Their age and health is a result of their practice, it is not that now they are old they take up tai chi ..... but don't despair, for it is not too late for us.

I could go on or you could just go and find out for yourself.

4. On attitude.

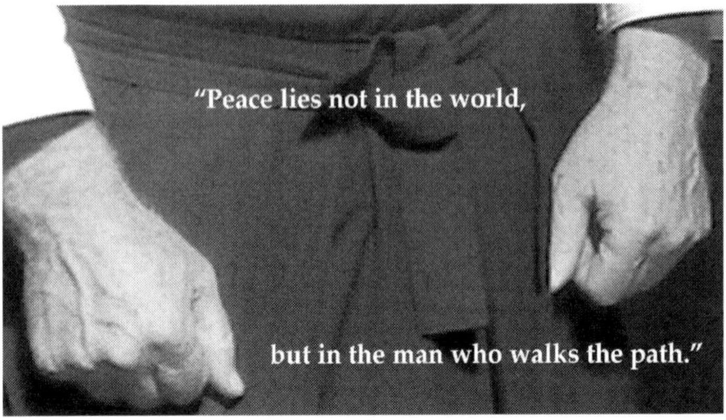

Trying too hard and wanting too much is counter productive.

'Take a step back and
you'll have much more space.'

How you use your mind makes all the difference.

'Whatever you practise,
over time, you become.'

Invincibility depends upon self,
vulnerability of the enemy depends upon them.

Your mind should not be inside, it must not be on yourself - it must be out there.

Beneath the surface is calm.
Yet in the calm is life itself and in the calm lays great power.
Therefore seek the calm - it's what will connect you to a oneness with the universe.

Change your mind - change your world.

*'Your body is the home you live in,
therefore, build a good home.'*

Find the balance between the defeat of your mistakes and the inflation of your successes.
The middle way is calm and relaxed.

Energy follows your mind.
All effective movement comes from your centre.

Relax does not mean collapse; consider using the word 'soften' in relation to a posture. Muscles, though 'relaxed', must retain tone and a sense of life force.
Try relaxing 'outwards' and feel the difference to relaxing inwards. Once found, you'll not want to return to old ways.

Opening and correct alignment of the spine is the way to have chi rise to the crown. Try to create this effect and when you do, you will know it.
No one said it was easy or that you would find it every time.
In tai chi it is often said that you should tuck in or drop down the tail bone and raise the crown of the head, keeping chin in by about a centimetre or so. However, even the very thought of relaxing and opening the spine to stretch it will cause tension. Therefore try this;- just **imagine** the spine is opening and stretching, almost like **watching** it happen. You should feel the subtle change in its relaxation and opening.
Chi kung strengthens the transformation of Chi through posture, breathing and imagination.
Because of the slow, flowing movements the body can relax, and in that calmness, external tranquillity becomes internal.
When you are centred, the tranquillity is projected outwards again.

Spirals - seek them out and actively exploit them.
Externally co-ordinate the limbs through the centre.
Internally co-ordinate intention, energy and consciousness.
Connect to the spine.
Be mindful of energy channels or meridians.
Learn to 'feel' each part of the body with your mind.
Keep hands at least one fist away from your body. (So as not to short circuit your energy field or aura).

If practised properly,
tai chi can only bring you benefits.

You can become more balanced, stronger and better coordinated too, while you enjoy a journey of exploration into and beyond yourself.
Until you are experienced, it is essential to listen to your teacher – this involves listening with ears, eyes and brain. Listen to your own body too, if in pain then stop and ask your teacher about it. Carrying out new exercises, your muscles are bound to be affected until they get stronger and you learn to relax more.
Tai chi will not damage you if done properly, but it might allow your body to access some old injury which tight muscles have hidden from you for years. Sometimes these old injuries come to the surface and it may take time to work through the problem so that you can better return to a more balanced body. Strange as it may seem, old memories are sometimes locked into our bodies and the sort of 'opening' exercises you will carry out in Tai Chi (or Chi Kung) can release the feeling and rekindle the memories – hence sometimes you might experience flashbacks or weird dreams for no apparent reason …… except now you do know why!

Your knees are particularly important for a healthy and active life – look after them – they only bend in one plane and one direction – so why would you ask them to do something else?

Watch a teacher's foot and knee relationship critically.

'Your body instinctively knows the correct posture, it doesn't need your mind's advice.'

**

5. The Tiger and the Goat

This is all about a change of feelings and about being body aware.
It is a tale for your imagination and hopefully an experiential journey through the mind and body of both Goat and Tiger.

A few years ago at an aikido seminar, I met and trained with a German therapist who effectively used animal Chi Kung as a method to 'cure' people of psychological trauma. This short article is not aimed at doing that but you may just be surprised what benefits you could discover for yourself. The more body aware you are, the more you will experience and any necessary changes will therefore be easier to find and make. There is a power available by mind association.

First, on body awareness; a little experiment; Look at the palm of one hand, think deeply about that hand and nothing else, stay relaxed and focused. It's almost like you are asking your hand what it is like to be a hand ... then listening attentively to its answer. You may feel tingling in the hand or warmth, heaviness or perhaps even a presence that you had never noticed before. If you are aware of such sensations, no matter how subtle, you should be able to meaningfully explore the rest of this article.

Let us suppose we are the Tiger, we have been frightened and chased by hunters deep into a wilderness. Our short lived, fear fuelled panic is over, the hunters are now far away and our tormented, mindless, crashing through dense woodland is a thing of the seemingly distant past.

We are completely safe, at rest in the shade of a great tree from which we have an easy and commanding view over a sunshine filled forest valley and the winding animal track that runs through it. We are at peace in our mind and our body is totally relaxed. There is no tension, complete peace, only the comfortable presence of soft and calm breathing for our companion; not even the leaves are stirring in the warm still air.
All during that day our erstwhile friend, the goat, has also had this same sense of peace, wandering through the small valley, stopping in patches of sunshine, feeling the warmth and eating at will.
Whatever the goat fancied eating, it did. The goat's sense of peace is at one with that of the Tiger's. Life was good, calm, happy, a joy to be at one with his own body and mind.
Oblivious to anything bad in his happy world, the goat walks the path, the path of his ever diminishing lifetime, towards the great tree. He has no mind of the Tiger, he has no mind for aught else but peace in his whole being. He knows no fear for he hasn't read this book!
Only you, suspect the tiger, the goat doesn't, nor does he suspect his life is only as long as the path he's taking.

Now let us return to our Tiger.
If you can, try and put your mind into how the Tiger might feel. Relaxed, breathing naturally, mindless yet awake. Feel that relaxed state in yourself, as though you are one with the Tiger. You may well think you are relaxed but often there is still further to go . . . relax your jaw muscles and relax your throat, feel that extra relaxation spread throughout your body. Relaxed muscles allow maximum energy and unrestricted blood flow. The Tiger (you) is at peace and as one with the pulse of the universe.

Now the Goat comes into view along the path.

As if you really were the Tiger, try and imagine the changes in feeling and focus within your body. The Tiger does not jump up nor become tense, instead the Tiger will gently connect all its muscles and its spirit as one, there is a soft but definite expanding connection throughout the whole body, there are no gaps in connection, the act of moving requires no slack to be taken up anywhere. The connections in the body are created by the mind . . . your mind. . . and not by tensing the muscle groups to form a structure. Any structure is counter productive and will slow response; instead, the relaxed connectivity provides an instant and speedy response to the Tiger's will.

You might experience a similar feeling by taking a gentle breath in and as you do so imagine your whole body gently expanding ... like a balloon does. Though expanding, it is still relaxed.

There is an awareness of the presence of consciousness in the whole body; mind and body have become one. (As they always were from the beginning of life.) The Tiger's eyes connect its soul and sinews in ownership of the goat. The eyes do not only look but they possess what they see. Just like you can see and 'own' a word at the end of this sentence, look at it as though the word belongs to you and you alone, there needs to be sincerity in your action and that you are infinitely connected with it, connected in spirit like the Tiger and the Goat.

(Own that last word with your eyes and spirit, feel what that means to do so.)

With luck and a bit of effort you will have experienced what it is like to be the Tiger as it spots its prey. This is all I hoped to share this time but there is always more. The Tiger will not move until its hunting distance is optimised, the goat will not notice until the Tiger moves. What of the sensations felt by the goat? Tension, fear, panic and escape if possible, they are the opposite sensations to those of the now hunting tiger but who had also endured such fearful feelings earlier in the day.

If the Goat did not run and encourage the tiger's prey instinct but stood its ground, not in defiance but with a sense of universal love, then perhaps the Tiger would not see prey any more and possibly once more the Tiger's feelings would change.
Life isn't always like that but there are occasions when it can be so for ourselves.
I hope you found something of interest in this experiment.
It is though, what **you** experienced, what **you** felt, that counts.

**

6. On partner practise.

Tactics in Tai Chi are to close the gap with the opponent, hence nearly all moves advance.
Most strikes use open palm - which is more relaxed and causes less injury on impact . . . to yourself that is.
Tactical advantage comes from the direction changes that occur in every move. . . this prevents the opponent from becoming either mentally or physically centred.

Follow the intention of the opponent, give up your own resistive strength, go with their force then take advantage when it is used up. Give up your fear of being pushed over - learn to let go and relax. Connect with your spirit.

When you have a partner, act as though no one were there, when on your own, act as though you have a partner.

If you try and predict an opponent's move then you have moved into the future and are no longer in the present, where something different may happen.

Be aware of and protect your centre, physically, mentally and psychologically.
In push hands; keep your structure. Don't let your arms cross the centre line.
Don't go back unless already turning.
If you just go backwards they will merely follow you.
Either deflect before their power reaches you or resist with equal power then deflect. Engage your chi.

You might relax but you don't concede - you merely relax down into a connection between them and your own centre.

If they can't feel anything, they can't do anything.

"A mind of 'no expectation' is required in a dangerous situation."

Empty force has limitations against an attacker but is good for healing. It means you are sensitised to the chi flow within you and in others.
Your mind needs to tangibly move through and in your body. Seek to improve your mind flow.
A punch goes from a big body to a small point. . . this is not the way of tai chi, which starts at a point and expands. Therefore, deflect and grow. Use Yi (*'ee'* mind)

Avoid striking an opponent with yang at the point of contact. . . use yin side. (Unexpectedly much more powerful and I believe used in the awesome Russian art of systema.)

When striking. . . including on your own pressure points for chi kung, use your mind on the **back** of the hand or your palm contracts which is not what you want, you need expansion!

The Tai Chi symbol is a circle ... no beginning and no end, no breaks, no straight lines. This is a wonderful image to cherish.

If you stop at any point then the enemy can adjust. Think back on the tai chi symbol . . . no beginning, no end.

Don't let their intent stay in your body but go in your mind where that goes.
(this is really very interesting but you might need help from someone who understands, in order to see it).

Be aware of and protect your centre. Your physical power at least resides in front of centre.

Analogy of water: - in pushing hands, if one person is resistant the other may 'flow' around this and reach the body.
Any attack must only be made at the point of change only.
Never exert all your energy, conserve some for necessary changes.
Know and understand your own body first.

The ocean teaches us the greatest of lessons -
No fixed part - no broken part - no beginning and no end - no linear - between the yin and yang there is no boundary - the peaks and troughs of waves are in harmony.

It is easy to be broken when all is in one direction.

Circular movements hide the beginning and end points of a movement.

Move yourself, not them.

All practice should have the energy exchange. . . not strength but energy.

Just like water, fast or slow does not come into the equation.

Techniques are like ocean waves. . . too numerous – but become water, and they are all yours.

Humans will struggle to deal with any move that has more than one direction at the same time, which is another reason why spirals are so effective.

**

7. 'The Gazelle and the Trampoline'

(One man's path to enlightenment.)

It was an autumn evening as the student set out for the long drive along lonely roads to the moors, and the isolated old farmhouse, where the master trained his secret knowledge.
The master, known as Sifu of Exmoor lived there with the gentle and lovely yogi, Persephone, a bright star in an often dark world. They shared their home and perhaps their secrets too, with a dog called Anubis, who had many friends – or at least thought she had.
So, it was dark, wet, and muddy on the track outside the farm, the student parked his car and put out the lights adding to the impending gloom. Out of the darkness came a white blur, even before his legs were fully out of the car, it was Anubis herself, speaking quickly in a language the student had not yet learned.
Later, after events had unfolded, the student was to reflect on what the barking language may have meant. He concluded that Anubis was excitedly saying, "Glad you could come. Tonight we're doing martial moves and you must be ready for the surprise attack; look, I'll show you," and with that, a full on 'animal paws' attack struck at his legs. "Come on," Anubis barked, "follow me.... and be ready!"

The student followed Anubis down the slope to the old farmhouse door from which Sifu of Exmoor had just stepped. Distracted by his master and not having understood Anubis' instructions the unfortunate student was ill prepared for the lightning speed double paw groin strike that was to follow, (apparently a favourite move by Anubis). Sifu of Exmoor laughed and demonstrated a simple mind control technique that looked very much like stroking Anubis' head .... Of course as students we know there must be more to it than that, probably highly refined transmittable telepathic chi energy or something equally impressive. Masters always tell us it's simple so we don't search for the real secrets.

The student pondered briefly; 'would he ever learn?'

After a while, others joined them in the great hall, but by their smiles and absence of mud in the groin area they had not received the secret training from Anubis. Perhaps he was the chosen one to be given such valuable if unpleasant private lessons from the master's dog.

Onwards then on our path of learning; First exercises from Yang and on to Hsing Yi adapted versions, all given code names so that the uninitiated would not understand if they overheard the training. "Okay," said Sifu, "after cat washes face move on to chicken."

"Can you show us the gazelle?" asked the student. "Later," replied the master, "these ones first then I'll show you the antelope," correcting the code word without making the student feel he had made a mistake – the mark of a great teacher.

Everything seems confusing, everything seems to have an opposite; when you rise something must fall and going forward requires some backward, but never too much or an awful event is manifested, known in the trade as 'double-weighted'. You must look for space on an ever increasing level ... but before you reach the limit, which is of course an unknown, you may have to act with power. You must not use your muscles for power but the body, however, in not using your muscles they must be relaxed, baring in mind that relaxed is not collapsed.

You must follow these principles even with a partner, whereby you yield without giving in and neutralise without them even knowing it, and then the power you have stored can be issued .... Providing it complies with the earlier principles of course.

While engaged in these activities it can help if you envisage yourself floating and suspended from a big rubber band in the heavens, and yet your *yong chuan* points (more code for 'bubbling well' – which is another code but in English) should be connected to the Earth, connected in a powerful but fluid way which is always light – despite that you weigh what you weigh regardless of how you think. There will always be stillness yet moving and in the midst of all your moving a stillness. Emulating a slow moving Gazelle between two trampolines begins to make it clearer for the novice. The Gazelle's ribs should go in the opposite direction of its skin and at the same time intention must be strong in the direction of action. The action is only transient depending upon partner reaction, the intention must be focussed and complete and yet at the same time be careful of going too far which may carry you into the forbidden world of 'double-weightedness'. Though your partner may move first, you have to sense this and arrive before them – and in doing so keep in mind all the above.

So this is the gist of basics and enough for one evening!

With thanks and farewells out of the way, the student returned home in the rain soaked darkness, enthused with new knowledge - all he had to do now was understand it.

"Mmm," he thought, and he clumsily gazelled himself into the kitchen and took a beer from the fridge. " Mmm."

8. On Breath.

A little more on breath;- why is it rarely taught and usually only to high level students? I have read that using the breath in the wrong way can possibly cause ill health .... seems a good enough reason to get it right I'd say. In general I have found that many students ask about the breath .... and as yet I don't have many answers ... I just repeat what I've been told when I asked the same question. 'Don't worry about it ... let it take care of itself'. Often though, an outward, expanding movement becomes associated with the out breath. Peng and Lu are both in breaths though, according to one Master in Shanghai ... and he could demonstrate why it was so, highly effectively. Another teacher said, 'do not show the breath to your opponent, for when they see this, they know when you are weakest' .... so there is much to learn about breathing ... but perhaps we are not yet ready to know these answers. Breathing in activates the sympathetic nervous system and breathing out, the para sympathetic.

[illegible] many wonderful breathing exercises of both a [illegible]ative and empowering nature and it is certain that [illegible]lowing the breathing rate to about eight breaths a minute actually changes brain chemistry. These exercises can be explored in meditations, yoga, chi kung (dao yin) and the like. In some you might be asked to hold the breath, my advice is not to do this in tai chi practice. Allow the breath to be natural to the event occurring. Counter to normal, relaxing on the in breath, balances breath and nervous system.

***

9. The Tai Chi Class and the Path to the Temple.

Spiritually uplifting, harmonic, Chinese music softly filled the air; students meeting once again as in the weeks before, chatting intently with each other.

The instructor never knew what they talked about – and to be honest never wondered either.

He clapped his hands loudly twice to bring the class to attention. Some students were always up and ready early, while others seemed to wait for the signal before they even changed their shoes. Some still chatted, seemingly frivolously and obliviously. When the instructor broke up conversations by moving the offending students to another space in the hall, the offenders would promptly start chatting to the new person next to them. Eventually they would settle.

'What's the point of shouting and rushing?' thought the instructor, 'it's not what we're here for.'

'We'll start this week with the Dao Yin exercise,' the instructor said from the front of the class, and from which position he could well see the grimaces of those students who obviously didn't like the exercise and the smiles of those that did. Trying not to let his psyche be affected by critical judgement on his plan, the teacher mustered his spirit and began the exercise.

Before the start, he once more reminded them, 'feet parallel; feet parallel; it's really important!' Occasionally he would spend some time correcting foot positions for those who weren't sure what 'feet parallel' actually meant.

It seemed that every week he had to repeat the same thing – he often wondered why – and even today, still wonders.

The Dao Yin exercises were completed to the satisfaction or not of the participants and in as many variations as there were students. The instructor continued the class with warm up exercises and form, wondering if he'd got it right too.

"It's more important to understand one move well and engage with the good energies and proper structure than it is to know lots of different shapes and forms," said the teacher, hopefully peering into a crowd of sometimes expressionless and unconvinced faces.

Did they make progress?

He could see that most of them did ….. in their own way.
He thought back to his own early, and inadequate, days of teaching, always desperate at the end of each class for some sort of feedback ….. 'That was a good class' ……. 'What a difference it makes when we do ..' …. 'I feel so much better after a class' … etc., but it rarely came. Now he was sure he was on the right track, he'd moved on, discovered things he hadn't dreamed existed before, and now feedback had less meaning any more – which was just as well, as not much came.

'Observation told the truth.'

The teacher turned towards the stage, put a CD in the player and pressed the play button. Suitable and appropriate music gently filled the hall. Now, suitable and appropriate it might have been but not necessarily to the taste of all the students. He remembered, once, he'd been asked to turn it off as it made the place sound like a cheap Chinese restaurant. Then there were the hard of hearing (including the teacher!) who it seemed insisted on standing near the music where they couldn't hear instructions – or stood at the back where they could hear nothing.
"Ah, meditative peace and harmony – that's what we're looking for," he reminded himself.

"The perfect man is spirit like, great lakes may boil around him, yet he will not feel the heat …….."

The teacher always had a plan, a theme, and an idea to pursue in his lesson. Of course, it was important to remain flexible and adapt any such plan. It had to cope with students coming in late and missing the essential pre-amble, which meant that the essential pre-amble became more an 'after-amble' in order not to rob latecomers of the best chance to learn.
He was minded of an old Vietnamese proverb,

"The man who only walks on sunny days
will never finish the journey."

"The Ho and the Han may be frozen up yet
he will not feel the cold ….."

"Feet parallel, feet parallel!" he shouted again as he wondered why most students left the instruction manual on operating their knees at home.

"Whole body. Whole body must be involved," he called out in vain as a few students operated their arms independently of their static straight kneed bodies.

And yet, how could he teach if he did not believe, and if he believed, could he perform?

If only he could put into practice the very advice that he gave his students. He called them students but really he saw them as friends sharing the same journey. He too knew what it was like to struggle with the new; to experience disappointment in realising that what he knew was either not enough or not strictly the truth he was really after; or to glimpse just how far away was the destination of enlightenment.

Yes, he knew the feeling, 'not internal enough', 'not co-ordinated', 'poor focus of intention'. He'd been there ….. He was still there! He didn't want to struggle to the top of the wrong mountain, or perhaps the right one but have no ticket to admit him to the temple, but at the same time, to give up was to remain in the valley of shadows and the abyss below.

Back to the class he would go, with renewed determination and yet one more cunning plan in his head. Drawing on experiences and ideas to make the class more entertaining and interactive he tried again. "Offer your wrist to the partner in front and when they tighten their grip use your body and not the gripped arm to move them," he explained as he demonstrated the advantage of this great 'secret' that was to unfold for the students.

Then it was their go. He would wander in amazement around the class, looking at all the variations, and give advice to each to help them conform. Then he would notice people in their pairs, talking. "How did you get on with the exercise, did you manage to do it?" he asked.
"Oh, yes," they would smile and reply in unison, "we've both had a go." (Like, one swallow does not a summer make, one go won't change the world either.) Then there were others who were still trying, but both gripping, and those with feet, independently blundering negligently out of parallel again, "feet parallel, feet parallel," he would plead, almost without hope by now. And yet there was progress. He could see individual students becoming energised and stronger; it kept him there.

"Thunderbolts may split the mountains and the wind shake the sea but he will remain unafraid ...." ...

As the music played and the students performed, his mind drifted to some other disappointments, to past students ....

'I once went to a teacher in Bumbling Town in Anyshire, he was better than you, you might know of him, his name was John. He used bits of card with North and South on ... and was very good.' (implying, 'not like you.')
'Perhaps you could draw out on paper the entire footwork sequence of the form; I think it would help me ...'
'Can we just do that bit again?'; Said as the caretaker waits at the door twiddling his keys and thinking of home and his dinner.
Then the lady who looked at her watch about every two minutes throughout the class, that's about 45 times! He didn't think she would return ... he was right.
"It hurts my knees!" Not surprising twisted like that; why not listen to the teacher's advice?
"Any chance of me buying a video of the Tai Chi?"

'Don't worry, please borrow my copy, and then bring it back.' (Ho. Ho! He wondered if they'd used the borrowed tape to over record Eastenders or something.)
Then the lady who told him at the end of a class, "I've not learned much off you; why don't you start a beginner's class?" (Translates as, 'why not hire this expensive hall and waste your time and money waiting for me to decide if it's worth coming to.')
He knew this and said politely and calmly, "The class is over now and we are just going to do a relaxing balancing exercise to close it down." As the other students quietly gathered in a large circle, the lady with all the advice on how to run a class, gained from her first and only tai chi lesson, stormed out to the main door. Now, the main door had a peculiar locking method, which she handled with as much success as she had with her tai chi, and so, now even more agitated, furiously stomped through the middle of the closing exercise circle and burst out through the emergency push bar exit and into the car park, where she no doubt found fault with everything else.

"Neither death nor life changes him; such a being he mounts the clouds, rides the Sun and Moon and rambles at ease beyond the four seas." *Nieh Ch'ueh*

He was aware that he and his students were in pursuit of personal growth, not an easy path, but for him there was also reward. It wasn't all bad; often he would see wonderful progress amongst many students, sometimes almost moved to tears as he witnessed the grace and harmony, the oneness and the peace of those who had found their own journey to the temple on the mountain. Smiles of thanks and hugs of greetings; it made it all worthwhile.

So, there you have it, a brief glimpse into one man's search for enlightenment – on a journey with his students; sometimes they too can lead the way.

He put down his pen and sank back into the comfy chair, eyes closing, he drifted into a dream .... at last ..... the top of the mountain .... the Temple of Enlightenment .... he entered in ... suddenly, a loud monastic voice broke the silence, "Feet parallel, feet parallel," "back foot, back foot," ...... he fell deeper into a sleep, his feet twitching in his new blue slippers.

**

10. On eyes.

I mention general points only.
When you look down (about 45 degrees) this can tend you towards relaxation, or worst case depression and eyes closed tend to internalise your feelings.
If you allow your body to follow the gaze of your eyes, then the body will flow without tension.

To be alert, look forward and out, eyes wide open, be the watching tiger. (This does not mean stare at a point or stare blankly; tigers would miss a lot of dinners that way!

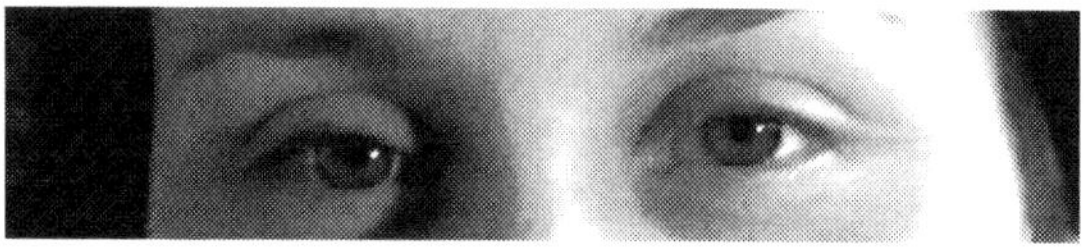

Energy follows the mind, therefore use your eyes in tai chi. The eyes lead and assess; use peripheral vision, which detects fast movement more quickly. Peripheral vision is aided by having 'soft' eyes. Soft eyes can be encouraged by imagining them deeper inside your head and looking out, through the skull as opposed from the front of it.

The tai chi principle of 'one thing moves - all move', applies to your eyes as well.

Exercise . Hold a posture, for example brush knee twist step is a good one. Focus your eyes with intent forwards .... sense the feeling. Now imagine your eyes are not at the front of your head but set way back in the skull so that as you look forward you 'see' from the back of the head. Sense the change.

Possibly you will find you are more relaxed and that there is a sense of being more behind the posture than in front of it.

You can but try.

The eyes should be softened, this improves peripheral vision but more importantly, if you allow it, it can soften the whole body too. Try it ... look ahead, even at these words, this page, now slowly soften the gaze ... do you not feel the wave of relaxation travelling through your body, are your shoulders not less tense?

In some ways there is a connection with the feeling at the beginning of a smile, the softening can travel the body, if you are patient enough to wait a while in the middle.

***

11. 'Away with the Fairies', in the land of Wuji.

Ye Olde English village Pub on the hill was crowded that night; and noisy too. In one corner, furthest from the bar, and engaged in more reverent conversation around an old wooden table by the inglenook, sat five men.

There they talked their favourite subject – Taiji – not for them the politics, the football or the price of a pint, but deep philosophical sojourns into the oriental internal arts. It had begun by one of them out loud revisiting the words spoken by a visiting Chinese Master;

"No Wuji – No Taiji!"

They took it in turns to speak their own, and no doubt borrowed, wisdoms, and then one amongst them, who had been absorbed in his own thoughts in a sort of day dream world, and oblivious of the noise and distractions around him, suddenly awakened his spirit to the conscious realm.
"Where've you been then; away with the fairies?" laughed one of his friends.
"Perhaps he's been in the land of Wuji," said another.
The laughter quieted and the younger but more wise of the group spoke; "Probably not, but who can really say. The translations from the Chinese indicate that Wuji means 'emptiness', but we all know that no one ever read any words penned by a writer, in the same way as the writer had intended; words are just too inadequate. I once had a dream that I will one day go through a doorway and know for the first time the great knowledge that I may well have already seen a hundred times before but never recognised. The occasion will only be meaningful because I entered by myself, in a state of open awareness, and for myself. We must each search for our own understanding of wuji – search with our own feelings and not with our thinking – then and only then will we know. We must walk the journey for ourselves; to be carried by another will only enlighten them, not us."

"To be carried by another will only enlighten them, not us."

He continued, "Perhaps wuji is to relax, as though in a dream; to relax outwards and not inwards as so many do. You know, when you see something truly amazing, beautiful, or inspiring, you see it more than just with the eyes but you see it with your whole body. Thought disappears and feeling and energy arrives."

Our friend, who'd earlier been away with the fairies, put his pint glass down and told them of one such experience he'd had. "It was coming down from Snowdon summit it was. I was walking with a lovely young woman who had just consented to be my wife; we stopped on a ridge that looked deep down into a cloud filled valley; the Sun was directly behind us, and there on the clouds below we could see not only our shadows but that they were surrounded by a magical circular rainbow. There was no 'want' any more, why should there be, because we 'had it'. Too much want can stop you finding your goal, we were lucky, we were not looking for this but it appeared to us in our aware and wakened state .... how lucky we were. We were absorbed by the vision, we reached out to the shadows with open arms, and they in turn waved back. Then the cloud cleared, the image was no longer in the 'real world' and we continued our descent, our bodies sensing much more than just the eyes had seen."

"Interesting, I wonder just how important the eyes are in wuji," mused another as he prepared to fetch another pint of local ale.

The man the group looked to for guidance on their path, edged forward in his chair and with elbows resting on the table he opened his hands in a gesture and said, "It's not just the eyes, it's what they connect with. Closed eyes tend us towards internalising, whereas open eyes can lead us outwards .... outwards to the universal. Eyes can trigger the opening of the spine and with open joints there is a belief that energy can flow, this creates a 'live' intent while the big muscles continue to relax. Eyes are the intention of your essence."

One, leaning back in his chair and who had been quiet before, spoke next, "A bit like George talking of the eyes of the Tiger, eyes that don't just look out at their prey but seem to draw the prey in – sort of see it and own it."

"I'm sure that comes in to it," continued their elected teacher, "eyes connect to the internal like that. The seeing trickles down through the internal, then that energy returns through the eyes. This will be sensed by others that observe you. Seeing may well be with the eyes, but there are other ways of seeing too. The whole body relaxes and becomes involved. Remember though, that the eyes are part of the one thing, and when one thing moves, everything moves, and when one thing stops, all stops; eyes are part of that too. You might catch a glimpse of some special feeling, and in surprise and pleasure you recognise the event with thought .... and the feeling disappears. The harder you attempt to return to that feeling the more illusive it becomes, perhaps lost forever as a once in a life time memory. Thinking destroys feeling, when all intention and thought are gone away then you will only be energy – Wuji." [*Author's note :- True meditative state.]*

Our friend, who had long been back from being away with the fairies, offered, "This place must exist, even though I've not found it yet myself; the yin yang theory bounded by the truths of thousands of years tells us this. Full circle we have come back to 'no wuji – no Taiji,' one is yin to the others yang and together they allow existence itself to be manifested, like, without two sides, the coin cannot exist."

It was late and time to go, last orders had been called, the pub now quieter with just a few die-hard locals left.

They all said their farewells and no doubt each hoped they would be closer to understanding by the time they next met; the door closed behind them and the night swallowed them up as they each took their own paths towards home, and who knows, perhaps towards Wuji.

Could it exist in the void of transition between yin and yang or is it the same as the emptiness in deep meditation?

You should ask yourself what you think about wuji.

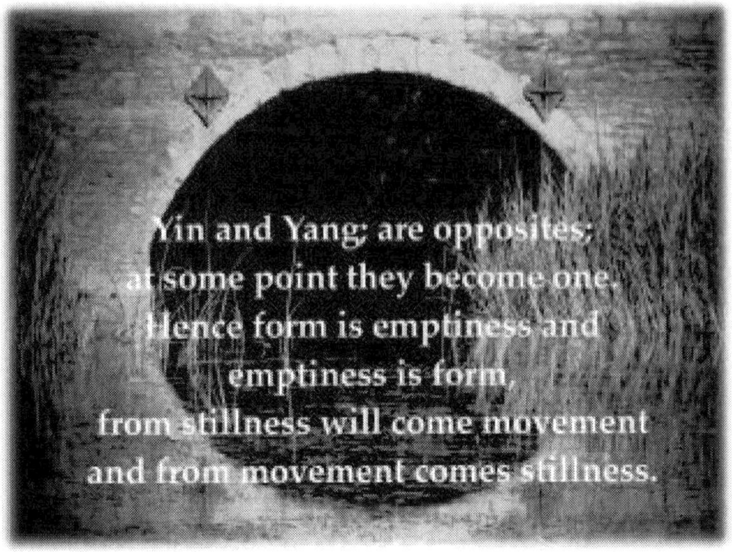

**

12. On Wuji.

'No Wuji – no Taiji,' he'd said. A few years ago I willingly accepted this statement from a teacher and I foolishly thought I'd understood it – I thought that all you had to do was stand in Wuji prior to initiating the 'thought' and the 'step' into tai chi form and as if by magic you have completed the bargain with the universe so to speak. Recently I heard the words again, but this time with new ears!
So, what is Wuji? I'd accepted that it meant 'emptiness''. Now I'm not sure what that means either. I looked on the internet for Wuji and found a few references, (some of which didn't even have what I wanted – it was merely a trap to put me in their sales site – how annoying, when you are hot on the path of enlightenment to be stopped in your track by a salesman). There wasn't much – unless you know different. I found this ....
"Wuji is the primordial state of non-being, a state of

nothingness and boundlessness or that which is without bounds or limits. Wuji, like the Tao, is and lies within all of the universe and in the human anatomy."

Okay, so now you have an answer and complete understanding eh?

My view here is that Wuji must be something such that if you could define it clearly in words then you probably don't know what it is. Perhaps it is something that we can feel, and if it disappears from our feeling only then will we know what it was – because we lost it.

In truth, I really don't know, however, that's not going to stop me trying to find out more – or writing something that may help others ..... Or not ! It's probably something (about nothing) that you will search for and may think you've found – but how will you ever know? (How would we know we've reached the edge of space, will there be a fence with a sign on it?) Trees must have the answer too; when moved by the wind they remain mainly still and yet when there is no wind and they look motionless they are filled with internal movement – they are growing all the time. – Movement in stillness and stillness in movement.

Is that stillness inside movement, our elusive Wuji?

My present understanding of the seemingly indefinable is that it is some sort of 'tangible' emptiness' (empty of what, we might well ask) and energy that can replace the structure created by our muscles as we 'let go' ; – Our intent, chi, and postural angles give us form. (We seem solid but we are mostly space anyway, with huge relative distance and space between atomic centres). It has been suggested to me that the emptiness is emptiness of blockage; and by some one else that the emptiness creates a space which fills with energy .... perhaps it is an active emptiness as opposed to a passive one. We might then reach a place where we are calm and still – yet full of the original life force; someone else suggested that like

a jar of settling muddy water with a light shining in the middle, so to our own light (energy) can also shine out as we relax the muscles.
When we practice our tai chi we should carry, in our movement, this quiet yet energetic emptiness (calmness) with us.
Mixed with the yin and yang of our tai chi is the primordial core of energy that was there before our world began – Wuji.

**

***

13. Meditation ....was it only a dream?

Outside, a lone honey bee foraged amongst the damp and fading blue Corn Flowers, and an unusually cool wind for the time of year waved the young, burgundy fronds of the Mimosa tree with an invisible hand.
Meanwhile, inside and arms resting on the old pine kitchen table, he was contemplating on how summer was more like autumn this year.

Steam rose from a mug of herbal tea as if it could compete with the playful smoke of burning incense, the little grey wisps of flying dragon smoke, playing all the way to the high ceiling. Notes on paper were strewn confusedly on the old table, chaotic, as were his thoughts.

As his mind quietened, he drifted off gently into a day dream and soon, sitting before him, were two elderly people. The woman had the semblance of being English of around the 15th Century and the man seemed of Oriental origin of no defined century, though by his clothes he'd led a frugal life. When they spoke, though the dreamer knew not their language, his dream intuitively allowed him to understand what they were saying.

The old lady calmly adjusted her shawl and gently placed her hands loosely clasped together on the table, "We understand that you wish to meditate; what is it that you wish to know?"

At last the dreamer had been sent the help he'd hoped for, for years, someone to guide him; "I don't know; how can I know the unknown, I don't know how or what to look for, yet I know I must look."

"Good, that's good," said the old man, "you're making progress just by realising that there is something there to understand; something; out there; something; 'beyond', something to 'believe.'"

Once again the old lady's calm voice commanded attention, "on your journey, though you must search, yet search not too hard, nor try too hard, you cannot 'make' it happen. But do not despair, for you can create the circumstances in which it is possible that it can happen. When it does, neither time nor space will exist for you, you will neither know how long or how far was your journey, but you will know something else, you will know something special for the first time. It is for you alone to find that something, only you. We have an old saying, 'he who is carried to the city walls will never know how far it was'. You may have heard it many times but was it your soul listening or just your ears?"

"Look, listen and feel my words," said the old man as he seemed to relax more and yet appear to grow larger, "I'm going to tell you something about words, but I'm sure you know already, it's just that you haven't recognised it." He continued, looking across the table from somewhere deeper behind his eyes, "We can hear words spoken by others but in your studies, you must surely have heard the expression, 'hearing is not hearing'. We may not understand these words or we may 'hear' with the thinking mind of our own knowledge what we thought they said and we 'think' we understand. In the beginning it is most unlikely that understanding will come with the words, though you may think for certain it has, this is a false dawn. It is possible, at this stage, you will find no real value in these words until an 'understanding' arrives 'uninvited'. When the understanding arrives, then the words will have meaning, a meaning from 'beyond'. Because we seek certainty, our minds may not be open to the new learning, which by its inherent nature is a process of change, a change towards what might appear to the unknowing as sheer fantasy. To help others, we try to use words, but they are a poor substitute. When an understanding arrives and you cannot explain it, and I mean the understanding and not its arrival, then you should know that your discovery is of real value, but it can only belong to you, the discoverer. Real truth is beyond all words, it resides in the pre universe ether – pure consciousness. No one can make it happen - it just happens. Let me ask you, 'do you think in words?' Do not reply, just feel the answer for yourself. Sometimes we do, for a conscious purpose – sometimes we do not and we visit a world of feeling and new discovery. We can become one with the sunset; we view it not with our eyes but our entire being, the Sun, the sky and you, each no different from the other; if the Sun could 'feel', then it would feel as you, all as one."
The dreamer couldn't resist speaking, "I can't help thinking, should I think or not think?" he asked.

"Look," said the old lady, moving some of the wordy notes out of the way and patiently leaning forward, "Words are only signposts on the journey, they are not the journey nor are they the traveller; so ask yourself, and don't speak this time, just how long have you been staring at the signposts and not been travelling? How many times have you known there was something you should do, but you don't? You, the traveller, must journey. Not to think, not to not think; if you are interested in meditation then thinking is good, but not thinking with words. It is a thinking you seek that exists not in the conscious world. Find that which manifests inspiringly from the silent thinking of the sub conscious, which for eternity has its roots in the infinite cosmos. Permit yourself some peace and a place in which to have it."
"Good advice, and much as in my own oriental culture," agreed the old man, "be comfortable, it is not through physical effort or will power, it is the something in the mind that opens the door, seek this first, only then will the portal appear and you have the chance, if you dare, to enter in. My ancestors used the expression wuji, - emptiness, when muscles relax but energy itself reaches out, the less your muscles do the further out your energy reaches, like a lamp in muddy water as the sediment settles the light shines out brighter, though the lamp itself was always that bright, always there. It has been said that we were all born a Bhudda but then we spoil it; know that the Bhudda still illuminates the deep within us, beyond the mist, the fog, the mud."

As our dreamer listened, he thought he glimpsed a hazy shape surrounding each of his unexpected guests, strange it was, something he'd never noticed before. As his conscious mind awoke to consider this event, like water through a sieve his guests disappeared from sight, nothing he could do would keep them, he tried and tried, but they were gone.
"But I still have questions," the dreamer thought - in words.

This dream was ended, he took up pen and paper, he struggled to remember and desperately scribble down the words he thought he'd learned, he slowly realised it was pointless, it was only words, there was no one who would understand, no one who would believe, why should they – he hadn't. ... only words ...... but he couldn't stop .... He picked up the mug to make a fresh tea ... the mug was still hot, the tea too hot to drink .... and steam gently rose with the incense smoke.

'To meditate, be the incense smoke.'

"Words are only signposts on the journey,
they are not the journey,
nor are they the traveller."

You can travel anywhere in your mind . .
. You just can't leave it there.

Reflecting upon illusion

14. One with the Universe.

It is well said, 'we are the map-makers of our own lives'. Not that we all, I'm sure, have not had the odd glance at plenty of other people's maps.

(Where are you going?
I don't know; where would ***you*** *like to go?).*

The older I get, the harder it is for my eyes to see the map, often it needs the brightness of a sunny day to help, but the easier it has become for my mind to 'see'. If only I'd known at the beginning, then my map would not be so faded in places, so crumpled and liberally festooned with frenzied alterations. There are a few crossings out near the bit that reads, 'Centre of the Universe'.

I'll tell you, if you want to hear.

"This is your hara," said the black belt Aikido instructor, pointing to a place just below the navel, "imagine that this place is the very centre of the Universe."

It was not so easy, but because I believed it had value I found it possible. By thinking that the Universal centre was within my own body centre it empowered me with a sense of calm and detachment from any dangers. It could take away fear. I was impressed. I marked it carefully on my 'map'.

For a while I would oft-times visit that place marked on the map and then, one day, I stopped going there. I don't know why.

Half a life time or more later, I visited that place again, but somehow it was different. I saw that there were now signposts pointing out. They point out, not just to nearby trees or views but out, really out, out to the seas, the mountains, the Moon, Sun and the stars – to infinity. All the signs point out – but peace dwells within.

Self becomes 'one with the Universe', not by pretending its centre is inside us but that wherever we are, centre or not of the Universe, we can reach out with our spirit, our mind, connect, and become one with it all – the energy we send out forms a conduit for that which we reach for, to travel back and touch us.

Like holding a hand out for a loved one – only by doing this can they too reach out to touch in the same way.

So the map shows not a concentrated internalisation but a vibrant viewing point from which our own centre can reach out, eyes wide open, to commune with the entire Universe.

If you can find this place on your 'map' you will surely find yourself at peace. Avoid engaging in conscious will, or want, or intention, merely feel the 'interest' in doing so – that is all it takes to invite a smile from the Universe. Be interested.

In this way you may find your world united in peace. In this place, find your body doing nothing except allowing the life force to keep you ticking over. In this time, know everything without needing to ask the questions. In this union you will be enlightened, you will become one.

It's what you sense that counts, perhaps the mind itself is neither journey nor destination. Perhaps the mind is only the ticket that admits your spirit to the temple of Oneness.

My latest thoughts though, need no map nor signposts either. Within us, every part of us, is space, the gaps between electrons and nucleus if you like.

On the far side of the universe, if it has sides, the very same space exists.

There is no difference whatsoever between the space there and the space here. They are one and the same.

Find the space within you and you will be one with the universe.

It cannot be otherwise.

[Quantum physics shows that 'entangled' atoms can instantly share the same event despite them being thousands of miles apart.]

(You should explore this question and feel the difference.)

15. On extension and pushing – the paradox.

Don't crowd your mind with disbeliefs - instead, believe - imagine - engage.

A paradox - or is it? The teacher tells you, 'never extend your arms fully.' Okay, so, in your mind you will have 'understood' what the teacher meant. Next week the same teacher says, 'always reach out with your arms, never let them shorten.' You nod your head and think you have understood, but there's that nagging thing in your brain that says, 'well that's not what he said last week. But in **his** mind it **was**.

Here is one thought on the subject. It depends on what is meant and what you understand about 'extend'. A straight arm is extended, its joints may well be locked up and therefore does not fit with tai chi principles. What about 'never shorten'? If you relax your joints and muscles but 'reach out with mind and finger tips', you can reach further than with tight muscles; the distance from the tip of your fingers to your shoulder joint must never shorten. This is not to say that you cannot bend your arm at the elbow - however, in doing this, the distance as measured along your arm from finger tips to shoulder must never shorten. This ensures that the joints are open, maximum chi can flow, maximum power is available.

Another paradox? The teacher says 'when pushing forward there should be an equal push backwards.' So, is he talking about an expansion in all directions, in which the forces are balanced? This would keep you centred and yet still have an effect on any person you push. It may also allow the body to be doing the pushing and not the hands. Oh no, so we are supposed to push with our hands in contact but yet not push with the hands, is this another paradox?

***'They are all confusing in the beginning,
later you will be confused at a higher level.'***

In fact, the more you can appreciate yin and yang and their placement the more you will be able to make of the above. Finding out more is part of your own exploration.

**

16. In pursuit of enlightenment – a shared tapestry of aphorisms.

It was a wonderful place to rest overnight. An ancient clearing, bounded on one side by a crystal clear stream that flowed musically through a deep wooded valley. Beyond the valley,

high snow clad mountains rose up to meet the occasional cloud in an otherwise clear sky. Even the valley itself was lost, lost in a world of other valleys and mountains which stretched beyond what the eye could see.
Two travelling companions, both with minds set on the path to enlightenment, sat by their camp fire, the smoke meandering through the autumn coloured leaves of the mighty oak and then skywards towards the heavens.
Aijin was the elder of the two by far and had travelled many a hard road in his search already; his young companion, Yufe, had been but a few years in pursuit of 'the great truth', the 'enlightenment', the 'oneness' that is foretold in the ancient manuscripts of all peoples. They travelled together because they believed they were on the same path, to the same place – though it is a knowledge no person can truly have of another.
Yufe was grateful for Aijin's older wisdoms and was never slow to ask questions, and questions he certainly had ... all the time. It was answers he needed, not questions. He reminisced briefly over an inscription he'd seen over an old temple door,

'If you leave not-answering I have no questions;
if you leave unquestioning I have no answers,'

it had given him many hours of pleasure – and not some little angst too.
However, Yufe's question was more simple this time, "Why is it, old friend, that the 'temples of enlightenment' are always up there, high up in mountains, so far out of common reach, why do you think it so?"
Edging closer to the fire and warming his outstretched hands, Aijin once again humoured his young friend and replied, "Well, it could be that to survive up there requires a special form of discipline to overcome adversity, or it could be that there, in that place, exists a simplicity with no distractions from our so called civilised society, or perhaps it is just to be closer to the great ether, the cosmos, or heaven as some might

call it. Me? I think it's more simple than that, I think we engage in the physical, kin to its twin the spiritual and, for those who can see, it relates well with the old saying, *'those who are carried to the city walls will never know how far it was'*, and there are many things to discover on the way too. Perhaps it is a metaphorical journey; perhaps it is not a journey of, way up there, but of a journey deep, deep down, down inside us, which is why only we can make it. Many would sooner climb a mountain than climb into their own mind."

Yufe too, warmed his hands by the fire and developed the conversation further, "Quite possibly so, I mean, when something comes to us too easily then we often don't value it as much. I hear that in China they have a saying that to be a hero you must first climb the great wall. I have thought on this and say, hero or not, the wise man will go where he wants, wherever that happens to be."

"Mm, I wonder, is that truly wise? Who knows what wisdom is? Come on, take a look at this and give me your opinion," said Aijin reaching for a piece of crumpled paper in his bag,

"'Walk with the man who follows the path behind him;
talk with the man who only speaks when
no one is listening'"

Su

"Ah, pass it over, let me read it myself, this may take a little understanding," said Yufe, and after only a few moments concluded that neither made any sense; he remembered an old saying, 'change the way you look at things and the things you look at will change,' "Now that's wisdom," he thought, "I can understand that."

Yufe looked at the crumpled note in his hand, and changed the way he looked at it, however, even as the seconds and minutes ticked by, what he looked at did not change, "huh, perhaps that's not so wise either," Yufe sighed.

"Mmm, who knows," said Aijin, "perhaps we would be wise indeed to accept what we have here; perhaps it is what we really seek but know it not as yet; fresh air, good food, shelter, warmth, peace and harmony; one with nature in a safe place to commune with heaven and earth. Will we find better than this if we move on?"

Yufe, the younger, deftly moved some embers with a crooked stick and pulled out some baked roots from underneath .... Mmm ... I'll let you know when I've eaten a couple of these," he chuckled, reflecting that it certainly was a good life so far. However, somewhere deep in the subconscious a mental note was being made to remind himself later that only those who risk truly live. Peeling back the charred Yam skin he mused, "You know, once we reach our destination there will be nowhere else to go; I mean ... a puzzle solved is a puzzle no more. What will we do once we arrive? They say a student has a thousand options, the master, only one. Surely it is also so with one who travels, and the one who arrives. We are on a journey to find an enlightenment that may imprison us in a certitude that there is no place more to find."

"Pah! You think too much, the physical may end but the spiritual not, for spiritual is of energy and can never be destroyed, now pass me one of those yams while there are any left."

Yufe passed the largest of the yams across the glowing embers to Aijin, "you know, old friend, you know that we seek to be one, ... You know, one with self, one with the universal and so on?"

"Yes," said Aijin, nibbling at the cooler edges of the fresh cooked Yam, "what's your point now?"

"Well, what happens when we finally achieve this oneness, how will we know?"

Spitting out a bit of burnt skin, "easy – you will recognise that you are one and in that moment all will be clear - the understanding of all past wisdoms will be revealed and doors to the future opened. You will have arrived at the beginning and recognise it all for what it really is."

“Okay,” said Yufe, fidgeting nervously, as some potentially uncomfortable truths dawned on him, “When I recognise that I am 'one', by inference, there must be two of me, the one that recognises and the one that is recognised .... You’re right, I think too much .... I often tell myself off about that.”

“There you are then,” said Aijin, with a broad smile, “if you talk to yourself then you must already have become one, and in doing so discovered you are two! You are therefore the enlightened one amongst us. Perhaps that is the destiny of us searchers, perhaps the great puzzle is answered by knowing we are each more than one. Do you not recall Kai Lung's words? That there are three of each of us; that which he is, that which he thinks he is, and that which he intended to become.”

Yufe stood to fetch some nearby soft pine branches, and so doing he spoke unwittingly to himself once more, “Ah, so much to discover .... so much to understand .... we are all students ...... to the end of our days.”

Returning to the comforting glow of the fire with his bundle, he noticed that his companion was collecting more fuel for the night time fire. “Nothing like using the 'now' to make a later 'now' a bit more comfortable,” Aijin smiled.

Fire logs neatly placed, and to the hoot of a distant owl, they both sensed that their journey for the day was nearly over. ...... Nearly.

As evening fell and the silent curtain of dusk drew a veil over the landscape, they both settled on cushions of pine branches and leaned their backs comfortably against a fallen giant; their feet and eyes alike looking contentedly at the fire.

After a while of fire gazing and silent contemplation, Yufe spoke of the journey they should make on the morrow, “we don't seem to be getting any where fast, do we?”

“'Be not afraid of going slowly, only of standing still,' says an old Chinese proverb; were we to go too fast then our souls would find it hard to keep up,” counselled Aijin.

"It seems a long way before we will even clear the valley, shame we didn't have a horse to take the burden," said Yufe wistfully.
"Oh you poor young wanderer you; finding the going hard eh? Don't you remember what I said earlier, that those who are carried to the city walls will never know how far it was?" Aijin replied sternly, admonishing his young friend.
"I thank you for your ever timely reminder, you have not only been a wise and pleasant companion but your words have taught me much of that which I would otherwise have forever been unaware. I thank you."
Aijin's reply was slow in coming, and in a quieter , assuring voice he said, "You are kind, but methinks misguided on this matter, for words are but a crude and ineffective tool, you may hear them a thousand times and you will hear them and think you understand ... and true, you may understand with the mind, but it will only be when you 'feel' the meaning that you will truly understand. Thinking is the enemy of feeling, when you are ready, and only then, the feeling will open the book of wisdom and you will read the story for the first time and know it."
"Well, your words have just opened the first page of my book, for I now sense the depths of something I saw many years ago. An old man, a nomadic monk of sorts, was sheltering in my village and often being asked by the villagers to teach them what he knew. He said very little, much to their annoyance. However, before he left the village, he had this to say to them, 'You asked many questions and I gave you no answers; for I cannot help you. To find the great truth you must seek that which cannot be taught.' Only now, all these years later do I sense that I have understood what he meant – but I'll try not to put it into words!"
They both laughed and enjoyed their laughter and enjoyed their knowing. They felt that a piece of the great puzzle had fallen into place, and no words were needed, or indeed, possible.

A yawn, a stretch, and another log on the fire and Aijin eased old bones into a comfortable position for sleep; -"I just hope I can walk in the morning – it's fine for you youthful ones, but my joints are a little stiff after a night under the stars."
"Well, sadly – or fortuitously – for we are who we are – and probably exactly who we deserve to be as well, we must make the best of it. I'm sure you'll be fine – we're not dead yet." Yufe yawned too, and was asleep as his eyes closed. Eyes too late for the flickering firelight to give away the secret flight of an owl on its silent way to supper.
Aijin, by an inexplicable quirk of habit against robbers, placed a small canvas bag of belongings closer by his side, not that there was anyone else within two days walk from their resting place. He muttered an old comfort that his mother had oft-times told him, "Child, anything that can be lost was never truly yours to keep," and with his mother's soft voice in his head, he was asleep.
All was hushed except for the sound of quiet breathing and the odd sharp crackle from the fire as it spat out a spark that began and soon ended its short life.
Now, lost far away in his dream, Aijin's nostrils widened with the scent of incense in the Jade Buddha Temple. Though he was one among many in the dimly lit and heavy timber beamed building, a powerful silence pervaded the throng. It was as though no one noticed that he was there, he watched as each person present performed some ritual before the statue, and after what seemed an eternity of meditation some of the monks stood and left, the great doors thudding, with a sense of permanence, closed behind them. The few that stayed behind, the chosen ones, the elders, the senior disciples, they gathered in silence to their master.
The master led them to one of the many ornate wall carvings and, unseen, slipped a secret catch that released a door leading into yet another windowless and timbered smaller room. Candles were lit and they filed in through the narrow doorway, following in the master's footsteps.

Still unnoticed, like a ghost, Aijin had followed them, and heard the door clunk closed behind him. How lucky he was, he was so excited, for this was the special day of days when the senior monks were told the great secrets and the history of their predecessors.
The Master pointed to ancient paintings on the wall, flickering candles illuminated the scene. "This is the foundation of our future," he said, "Here the founding monks began the building of the first temple – and in this very room, in which we stand together now, they too stood together then. Know you this, you are all free as of this moment, you may all speak, you may ask any questions – please do not waste this freedom."
"Master, these figures, here, is this the tai chi that they practised?"
"Yes it is, but in a form now long lost, even to us, though through their practice it is recorded that they found a sense of peace and detachment that to them was never lost and always valued, hence the rare expressiveness of their postures."
Another spoke, "And what of this, master, this symbol next to the Buddha?"
"An ancient symbol; again lost to the world except for this place and now to you. You ask now, and it is indeed about 'now'. The picture shows the Buddha exhaling and holding the out breath; on the long awaited in breath the Buddha experiences the breath of life itself and its existence in the moment, in the moment of 'now', beyond and before which nothing else has as much value. The symbol you mention is ancient and means, 'now and eternity are one'. On this matter, you must think for yourself, though it is similar to an exercise in your own practise, to know it truly may take you longer than your young years."
A tall man near the wall held up his candle, "and Master, what of this picture that appears to be the night sky, in which little streams join to make a river, a river that cascades in a

mighty waterfall into a great lake where it spawns stars, planets and moons of its own?"

"You chose wisely in your search," the master smiled, "this signifies that nothing is original that didn't already belong in the great Universal of the beginning. All words and all wisdoms of men were written in the stars and though many think they are the first, it is not so. All knowledge is pre-written in us before birth and it's up to us to find it. We all know already, it is just that it has not yet become visible."

The candlelight reflected both on students and Master as one, and he continued, "It has been aptly written that, 'sleep is the watering place of our soul, to which it hastens at night to drink at the source of life,' when you meditate you can become one with this mystical river and it will show you how to see these wisdoms – if you let it do so in a silence of your own, for how can you hear the river when you make so much noise yourself. Listen to the flowing river, for it will bring you many answers, and both at the beginning and the end they will be the same .... But wait .... Something disturbs our journey.... I sense that there is amongst us one that does not belong ...."

As the Master scanned the candle lit faces, our dreamer was filled with the dread of discovery, - in one short moment a strong hand gripped his shoulder, he tried to escape but no amount of effort would make his cowering body move, try as he might. The sound of a man shouting at him filled his ears and his mind – he fought desperately in his mind to realise where he was.

Yufe took his hand from Aijin's shoulder, saying, "Welcome home from your nightmare, it seemed to last forever and I feared I would not wake you."

Aijin slowly began to relax his taut muscles and freed his joints, "What a dream, if dream it was – so real – such wonder – I learned so many secrets in the temple."

Now both fully awake, Yufe implored Aijin to tell of his new found secrets.

"Well it's really strange, I know I learned great things but I can't exactly tell you what, I don't have the words, it's all unclear now really .... perhaps I'm not yet ready – that's why I was found out ..... I do know that the river has answers for me .... for us .... for all of us ...... but how will it tell us? I wonder if having seen the Temple, it will never be shown again, perhaps it was only a vision, a tool, to show me of its existence .... I'd like to go back .... but I think that the door, the secret door, will no longer be opened for me – it will never be the same again - I'll have to open it myself next time ... yes, that's it, I must find the door for myself, and enter in."

Early forest mists were now made visible by the rising dawn, Yufe blew on the ashes of the fire and it breathed into life again, he looked up satisfied, "I'm sure you'll know the answers, they'll be in there somewhere, let me know when you find them."

"Aha", said Aijin, "of something I am sure, that you must walk to the city wall yourself, by me carrying you, you will not find your own answers, you would be a prisoner of another's words and never find the great 'freedom' that you seek. I will tell you what I discover but I think you will find them empty words till you become the discoverer or, perhaps, the discovery itself."

"Mmm, I sense you are right, I have seen many times a secret discovered and passed on to those that had not sought; I saw that they heard the words but they carried no value to them, they had not endured the journey that makes the view worth while."

They, as was the awakening forest, were now fully engaged in the new living day, and all three of them, or indeed however many of them they might be, were to rise with the Sun and live with the Sun till dusk would find them walking their path once again.

How long that took was up to the Earth and the Sun but how far they went, was up to them. They were their own destiny.

'To find the great truth you must seek that which cannot be taught.'

**

Whatever your belief, beware, because it is you that lives in it.

***

An artist's skills reveals perfect posture.

17. On physicality

As a general rule your eyes will look to the leading hand, thus training you to look where an opponent might be. With your hand just below eye level it equates with looking at the opponent's chest.

Never underestimate the value of hip joints, ever!

Focus your mind on your centre of gravity.
Keep your back straight and turn the waist (hips to neck) - The parasympathetic nervous system is stimulated.
Relax all the muscles and bones in your feet and ankles. This leads to greater relaxation, stability and grounding as your connection with the earth improves.
Keep all joints open - that's all of them, always. You may act out a closing posture but the joints will never close. You must sense the expansion - the reaching out.
No leaning towards extremities ! In any direction. Follow this rule for more effortless and sensitive balance.

Stepping will often be like a cat, or walking on thin ice, check the ground before your weight transfers. This enables you to withdraw the step at any time yet retain balance and control. Remember that you would normally be stepping to the side of your opponent, therefore place your foot accordingly.
When you push a ball. . . it all moves. So it should be with your own movement.

Pay attention to the joints, for it is through them that energy must transfer from one part of the body to another.
When moving through a posture, if you can 'bounce gently and feel the energy hit the floor and rise again then the energy is not locked in your joints. . . a useful little test of posture.

Keep hip joints free and knees in line with toes.
Keep all joints open and the chi will flow.
Be mindful of the dynamics of the dominant hand and foot.
Mind guides body, body follows thoughts.

'Quietness is the guide to movement,
stillness comes before motion.'

When posture is balanced the body is centred and stable.
Be aware of the eight directions .

Never hold your breath.

Flowing like a river, allow your joints to release and your muscles to stretch.

Legs always slightly bent.

Continuity is essential. Use circular approach, internally and externally.

'Your arm may bend but never shorten'

Your arm should stay as one with your body; if isolated it becomes weakened and vulnerable.

When you bend the knees the joint should not close; in fact it should feel like you have no knees.

You can imagine that you are encompassed by a sphere of energy and when you move, it all moves with you, and you never let a part of your body protrude beyond its boundary. These pictorial ideas may be one key to discovering the feelings for good tai chi and advancement.

Relax the bones and muscles in your feet. Open your foot - feel the connection with the earth. The middle of the ball of the foot, *yong ch'uan* point or bubbling well, the only place you should feel your weight.

Learn to feel the air with hands and arms.
Be sensitive to it and feel it when you do the form. Think of 'wave hands like clouds.'
Be smooth and relaxed.
All movement continuous as is breath.
Circular movement.
Absorbed, concentrated mind.

Completeness - each movement uses whole body.
General principle - shoulders over hips (later they become one)
Wave hands like clouds - have light feet.
Tai chi movement arises out of stillness, and returns to it.

The interplay of movement and stillness are crucial to your tai chi. . . they **are** your tai chi.

Major energy pathways pass through your joints, therefore any tension restricts this flow. . . relax and open all joints.

Always the same order of flow. . . hip knee foot, shoulder elbow hand, regardless of direction.

Don't stand on heels as the bone is hard on the earth and the energy is sent back into the body. Use the pressure point, *'yong chuan'* (soft part of ball of foot) so that you can cushion the body.

The body should feel like a boat on the water.
When you want to turn make sure the boat is not in a trough but on the crest.
When standing on one leg have a sense that each time, you are free to kick with the other.

Never let their force meet yours.

Making the first step in Tai Chi - **literally**.
One thing is easy – you step with the left foot first; unless, of course, you know different. I have yet to come across a variation from left foot first. I read some while back in a Tai Chi journal, reasons why we use left foot. Without going into a rewrite, it seems that for most of us our right leg is stronger, all marching starts with the left foot too for the same reason.

How do we make this step? One of the first teachings I remember was, 'when you step try just to move your hips across smoothly to the left.' Next came, 'lift the left heel first; slowly, as the toes become the last to leave the ground, the left leg will feel light and the right leg strong and grounded.'
So, there's a couple of things to try.
One teacher said, 'right, let me see some tai chi.' I began the first step ... he said, 'no, start again,' as I returned my left foot to centre he said, 'that's right, that's the way.' I must confess it took me at least three goes before I understood what he meant. Try it yourself ... so much thought and effort goes in to making the perfect step that it interferes with the smooth and natural step that you will surely make when you say to yourself, 'no, start again'; with no pressure your left foot just returns – without thought!
That's what he wanted.
Another teacher revealed his understanding by saying, 'accept your body weight into your right leg, the more you can do this then the lighter the left becomes, and almost steps for itself.'
Do you step left in a straight line or is there a circular element? Well, if we accept that there are no straight lines in Tai Chi, then perhaps we should see how we can make our first step true to Tai Chi.
Lastly .... so far, anyway ...... I read in a Wu Style Tai Chi publication from the 1980's the following:- *'stand naturally, feet together, arms hanging down in light contact with outer sides of thigh bones, tips of middle fingers pressed against the middle of the thighs.Top of head erect, tip of tongue in touch with hard palate, eyes looking horizontally ahead. Weight evenly distributed between your two feet. Relax all joints, loosen all muscles. Maintain tranquillity.*
Keep top of head and body plumb erect, eyes looking forward – shift body slightly to right, and think tip of nose to be vertical with right toe and coccyx vertical with right heel. At this time the left foot will move naturally sideways by shoulder width. Weight now on right foot and mind on tip of right little finger. Right side of body tensed, left side is relaxed. .... equalise weight on both feet.'

Keep the spine open and free and you'll not go far wrong.
So, perhaps this will help you make your first step eventually.

A new idea from Longfei students on the 2010 China trip ....
Though your right, standing, leg be ever relaxing, feel also it ever expanding. Worth a try, as you do this, the left foot seems to ease off the floor on its own, ... most interesting.
And one more idea too ..... as you sink into the right leg encourage your right kua (hip crease) to open more, (sort of trying to raise the right ribs .. but not really) You should find that the weight seems to disappear from your standing knee and the lifting leg seem to lift of its own accord. Strange but true.
And more recently - prior to stepping, open ming men and imagine the hips rotating to bring the thigh muscles forward and around. You should now find the step very easy to make . . . and your whole body remain connected too. You do need to have body awareness, moving your consciousness about is a requirement and at some point you need to be able to do this.

'There are no secrets to which
you cannot find the answers.'

**

I believe that when you read or hear the explanations of masters and you sense an understanding beyond their words, then you are walking your own path - you will have discovered the true way.

***

18. Keith's Sheep and the fence.

"Now," he paused in thought as he scribbled his notes in the *Royal Hotel* while awaiting his roast dinner, "is it Tony's or Persephone's fence?"

It had all started to meander through the confused neuron fields of his mind a few weeks before: - the usual gang were in their favourite pub after tai chi class. He couldn't remember what had sparked off the conversation, but it went a little like this. ...."You have to search, but if you look too hard then you don't find what you want; it's another paradox really, but the very act of 'want' hampers your discovery – want is the fog that hides the path."

"A bit like sheep wanting the grass on the other side of the fence," he offered.

Keith, knowing just a bit about farming, supped his real ale and said, "and do you know what? ..... as soon as they're the other side, their first thought is to get back again!" The image made them laugh and they returned to their crisps and beer.

Not so very long after this event he was visiting his mentor and distant teacher, Tony, and mentioned the conversation. "Ah," said Tony, "interesting. Now, using your mind, visualise what it is you want, just like the sheep see the grass, and in your mind approach the 'fence', calmly and with patient consciousness. When you arrive at the 'fence', imagine that you can remove it, and in its stead there will be a space, a gap that separates where you were and where you wished to go. Enter that space using your mind, your imagination. In this space all is connected, physical and mental all become one; at this point you should find you are one with all, one with the universe – your search is over."

"Wow," he thought, "I can sense the value in this," and his neurons raced to create a memory of this mini enlightenment.

Later that night he was to put the theory to the test. His mind was so active, what with the day's journey and new information, but he needed to sleep. Sleep was where he wanted to be; the more he wanted some sleep to calm and refresh him, the worse the fence became. In his mind, he approached the fence, and surprisingly found the space; he entered the space and sensed that all became quiet and still, and sleep crept ever closer – that is until he thought, "Hey, this is working!" and he was back on the 'wrong' side of the fence again.

Morning came with a light fenland mist and, after breakfast, they drove to the workshop venue on 'Synergy and Healing' and all was soon under way.

He made a mental note to use this idea next time he meditated, 'Mmm, a nice idea,' he mused, as he returned his attention to the class. Tony was explaining how best to approach clients and chose to illustrate it with a story about a pet dog with an injured paw. "You want to help the dog," he said, "you must approach calmly, with whole body, not just your hand. In the brief instant of the first touch a moment exists when you and the dog are one. (The space where the fence once was) but this connection of oneness can pass quickly and now Ego and you are the 'great healers' and dominating the situation as you 'will' your energy to, 'fix that paw'. You are no longer 'one with all,' access to the great universal has slipped through your hands. When you are connected to the great universal, there is no fear, no want, and in that place of nothing, everything is yours."

Later that cold winter evening, as the car hastened homeward and the long road rushed under the wheels and backwards into a deepening darkness, he sat still, warm and comfortable in the middle. His mind wandered pleasantly around some recent teachings he had read;

'Be of good heart,' went the voice in his head, 'and begin a smile' …… "That's it," he thought, "the beginning of what we want is actually found in the middle, it's not at the beginning nor at the end. It's not the straight face nor the smile, it's that

little bit of relaxation in the middle where it all happens, just before the smile – just where the fence was."
Many miles and hours later, while visiting friends on Exmoor, he spoke of his new found wisdoms and how he had tried to share them with others, but how he had failed to make them understand – for it meant nothing to them.
Persephone sympathised and offered another glass of mulled wine, "perhaps," she said, "it is we who put the fences there, if we were not to build them perhaps we would intuitively be one with the universe; perhaps the gap you speak of is the place where something greater than we exists, the very thing that allows the healing to be manifest.

Drinking down the warm mulled wine, he wondered if we can ever stop building fences, only then, perhaps, we can really help others.

Whose fence is it, Tony's, Persephone's, or is it yours?

How many have you put up while reading this?

**

'Want is the fog that hides the path.'

**

19. The Chair, the Flower and the Rabbit.

Treasures from the Tai Chi road.

If I could but write this well, you might understand it, but even if you understood it, it will remain a flawed gem until you can 'feel' it. However, I am driven to try. I hope you too will be driven to find this same treasure. These are the treasures in life that no other can steal, so you need not hide them behind barred doors. In fact, your own treasure is the greater if you give it away.

As we small group of students sat in the old farmhouse enjoying an after training glass of wine with our teacher, I tried to remember those little gems that I had picked up in the class. No doubt you have been there too .... 'wow, what a brilliant idea that is, I must remember it for later,' then, when later arrives, all you can remember is that there was once, and not so long ago, something that you knew was great and which you had intended to remember. I sat, sipping the wine and delving deep into a memory only an hour old, at last two words came to mind, rabbit and chair, but I knew there was a third, then it came to me, 'aha, of course, flower.' I struggled to hang on to the words while more interesting conversations continued around me. These words were needed to trigger a chain of thought that creates feeling;

the feeling we hope will remain
when the words are long gone.

The Chinese internal arts are littered with vague aphorisms, almost uninterpretable inferences, and poetical imagery that are supposed to enlighten you; and they will, if you only knew what they meant.

An quick example in story form.
"Our teacher says we should use the magpie bridge."
"Oh, and where's that then, in town?"
"No, it's a connection in your mouth that you make with your tongue."
"Are you sure he's not having you on? Perhaps it's a word, the meaning of which, has been lost in translation."
"No, for sure that's what he said; it's supposed to create an energy loop in the body."
"Oh .... and what's it feel like then, this maggie bridge?"
"I don't rightly know, I don't believe in that sort of thing; but he said, that if we did it, it would change how we felt, and that it was more than technical, it bordered on the spiritual.... I'm not so sure though."
"Oh?!"
Now, if these two had felt the 'magic' of the Magpie Bridge, they would no longer doubt – but how are we to feel it?...... that is the question.
Okay. Now, back to the chair, the flower and the rabbit. Amazingly – or perhaps not so – you must find out for yourself. You cannot be told or shown by another, no different if you wished to play a musical instrument ... does it not require practice? Yes, you need a teacher to put you on the road, but it is you that must walk it – the easy going and the rough. If you don't walk the road you don't go any where, and as you no doubt realise some of the most beautiful scenery is only accessed by walking. (No cars to mountain tops or crystal caves or jungle temples, only feet to take you there ... your own!)
From here on, if you don't intend to try and 'feel' the advice and to 'feel' the stones of the road under your feet, then do not read on. Stop here, for it's not your journey.

You may have bought the map but
it'll likely stay on your shelf.

For the tai chi student this opening move will be familiar; feet shoulder width and softening the kua (hip crease), bend the knees. Feel how that is and then relax and come out of the posture while reading on. Imagine you are about to sit in a chair, just before you actually release your body to the chair there occurs a little relaxation of your own body.

It is this feeling of relaxation you must seek to feel the next time you open the first Tai Chi posture.

Give it a try – or two – or three – the road is long.

Should you discover one of your joints is tight and uncomfortable there may be many things you could try – this one's not bad. Feel the joint in question with your mind, see it as a flower bud – with your mind, feel the flower gently opening, steadily, smoothly, inexorably expanding, unstoppable – feel it happen, feel the tension go.

Still with me? Ready for the rabbit? Well not so much the whole rabbit, just its ears. You can take a tai chi or chi kung posture if you wish or even sit comfortably for this one. Try and quiet your mind, then when you feel ready, (that's feel not think), imagine you have rabbit's ears, lovely long soft rabbit's ears sticking up above your own. Got that? Imagining them? Right, in your mind feel the tips of those lovely ears, sense what it is like at those tufty little ends. If you are not laughing by now, and that's good for you too, you should feel a change that trickles down through your body and at the same time feel that you have extension beyond body.

Even in the Appledore pub as I write this, I can feel the rabbit's ears – I just hope that no one else here can see them!

Go on; ask the rabbit, it may know more than you think. Two warnings here; One, the rabbit's answer will only lead to more questions. Two, don't talk out loud to the rabbit, especially in the pub.

May your road be happy, full of flowers and rabbits ... with an occasional bench.

20. On Philosophy.

Can your own mind make you ill? Most people believe this.
Can your mind make you better? Most people doubt this.

'Here... stillness is real, movement an illusion.
Now. . . silence is real, sound an illusion.'

Be realistic in your expectations of change.
Do not be in a rush . . . do not over water the seedling!
The chi flows and tells the body to act.
Let consciousness be the guide for all body movement.
Concentrate and engage with the imagination.
Important to do it right, not quickly.

Changes in the natural world are infinite and the tai chi symbol is a guide to their understanding.
Translators always lose something of the natural essence.
Why is it so difficult to engage the 'now' ? - because all thinking of the progressive mind is done past and future, we are not trained in thinking in the present.
Change your mind - change your world.
'Take a step back and you'll have much more space.'

Your body is where you live, therefore, build a good home.

Tai chi creates in you a sense of something you never knew you lacked.

Sometimes we glimpse a 'knowing' but forget where and how we came to it.
Seek out all circles and spirals and mindfully exploit them. Sometimes they will not be what or where you think they are, therefore search diligently: - some of them are internal, therefore not seen - only felt.
Extremities are extended to the infinite.

Keep your mind open, do not be imprisoned by your own thoughts.

"Don't spend your life decorating the walls of a prison you built for yourself."

Simon.

Keep control of your own destiny.
Tai chi is not just about moves, but about beliefs.
Breathing is a continuum, like dusk is the junction of night and day, day and night.

***

**

21. Can it be true, that we've more power when we relax?

(I believe you will gain most from this article if you take your time with it ... as much time as you need .... Pause at places of interest ... then continue when ready ... all in your own good time.)

By more 'powerful' I mean, better recall, greater physical ability, co-ordination, balance and resistance to external pressure, better immune system, more discipline, better tempered, less pain - both physical and emotional.

In tai chi the Chinese call it *'song'*, to relax; and the tai chi masters will repeat it to you over and over. Therefore we must presume it has great significance. The tai chi version of 'relax' may well be different from your own understanding of the word, and we'll look at that later in more detail.

Many, if not all, 'therapists', including traditional western practitioners, want you to be relaxed, and to this end they provide you with a comfortable chair, couch, surroundings and sounds, and sometimes incense, to bring this about. Often you will be left 'to relax' before and after, "please get up slowly, take it easy for the next, 5 minutes, 24 hours, 30 years!" Why? Possibly because it is part of a greater, natural, healing process. Probably your own. After all, when injured or sick the body's first plan of action is to lie down .... and relax.

I am content to believe what I have read about the benefits of the meditative state, which can include yoga, tai chi and some gentle exercises, which activate parts of the brain where endorphins are released and where the dopamine pathways operate. When in the positive state the nerve chemicals and hormones released have a helpful effect on your immune system. (Practising chi kung has been shown to improve the T cell, - white blood -, count by up to 40%). Compare this with the effects of a stressed body which produces Cortisol which is an anti-inflammatory and lowers the immune system's ability to fight infection or heal wounds etc. Limiting the stress response is important to our health, e.g. in controlling arthritis.

Tai chi and similar arts also aid control of breathing and encourage slower, more effective, heart beats.

What do we understand by the word itself? Perhaps synonymous with relax are ... soothing, calm, peace, power.

Why power? To relax gives you power to live in the rat race, but remain unaffected, surely that is **real** power. Ever lost something, gone into a panic, stressed yourself and cannot, whatever you do, find it? Then perhaps even weeks later, in a period of true relaxation, that 'eureka moment' strikes and you know exactly where to find it. Wouldn't that have been of more use earlier on?

Stress is an unwelcome and frequent visitor that will turn up without you asking. Not so? Just feel the tension in your neck and shoulders as you read this, and it sneaked in on you uninvited. Relaxation is one of those rare visitors that must receive a proper invitation before it will arrive. We cannot normally 'hurry up' to be relaxed, can we? "Come on, come on you, ... relax. ....Come on hurry up, I've got a .... Bus to catch, ... dinner to cook ... garden to dig .... Oh, blow this; I can't wait all day for you to relax ..."

Mmm, that doesn't seem to be the sort of power that interested us earlier, does it? Instead, some rat race stress has been allowed to have power over you and how you feel and live your life. Nor is it the amount of willpower you can bring to bear, but the quality of mindfulness, and even belief, that counts. Your beliefs are the reality in which you live. You are, indeed, your own destiny. You chose to pick up this book; you chose to read thus far;

you alone will choose what you do next.

There are lots of good exercises that may help us relax, physically, mentally and emotionally too. I suggest you explore a few so that you can discover the idea of 'power' connection for yourself.

I'll offer you a simple exercise to try if you wish, then I would like to tell you about the '*song*' (relax) of tai chi.

Please give this a try, you have little to lose; make a stern, even cross, face... you can do it now ... unless you need to leave it till later when not in the public gaze! Okay, so what did your body feel like? If you are body aware you will have felt the tension in your chest, back etc. Now change it for a smile .... Feel how the whole body joins in and relaxes? Smiles are contagious aren't they? Okay, another stage. Be grim faced again and then smile ... but this time not so quickly. Please go so **very** slowly from grimace to smile that you may observe the tiny moment of relaxation which you must pass through to get to your full smile. Go **slowly**, look **carefully** for that tiny bit in the middle, in that space the power resides. Now try again, but no need to go all the way through to the smile just find and hang on to the relaxation before the smile itself ... now feel that relaxation and calm trickle down throughout the whole body. Lovely, and in doing so you have taken the first steps to power and a better immune system.

While we are on smiling, this too is a lovely exercise, costs absolutely nothing and won't get you locked up unless you do it too often in public! (Smiles release endorphins and serotonin into the blood stream. Both are beneficial).

Make a smile, it doesn't even have to be real, now, with mouth lightly closed, ease the tongue back so as to gently restrict your breathing a little, and both physically and mentally very slowly breathe that smile down, deep into your body. Relaxing?

You may well be confident that you are able to relax at will. Give it a try now and if you feel that you are fully relaxed, test it out either by relaxing the hairs on your head, or relaxing the throat. Did you feel that this took your relaxation a little way deeper? Experiment with the ideas, and guess what, more relaxation will come your way and all the benefits that go with it.

Now to *'song'*, the Chinese word we interpret as *relax*. Note that this version of relax does not mean 'collapse'; it relates to a place in the middle where space exists, a space where power resides, it is empty of tension and full of energy. The Chinese believe that the Chi, (very loosely we can call it energy), flows between muscle and bone; in order to maximise chi flow the muscles must be relaxed to a point where, should they relax any more, gravity would cause that part of the body to fall. Muscles relaxed, yet filled with life force, joints open, the 'empty' space between filled with energy, and mindfully directing the chi, maximises the flow. The flow of Chi can be experienced by seeing the hands darken with increased blood flow and sometimes a warming or tingling feeling.

We are all subject to the influence of energy, wherever we are, we have no choice, it's just we may not be aware of it. Try and make connection with this energy, utilise it, take charge. By this connection we travel towards better health and longevity.

An analogy; an electric socket with all its power is of no use unless you can connect to it. Behave in certain ways and you improve the connection, soften the body, and calm the mind (spirit). Remember, nothing can be forced, 'calm' is the plug for the socket.

So, come on, relax and feel your own innate power.

The above still represents my current beliefs based on what I have seen, heard and felt and is rooted in the teachings of others to whom I remain grateful.

**

22. Cramp cures for the tai chi student.

(And any one else interested)

Most people will accept that acupressure and acupuncture, when carried out properly, can relieve pain and promote recovery. Thousands of people can testify to this truth. The same pressure or energy points used to heal can harm as well, so it is best if you know what you are doing, though you shouldn't be able to cause yourself too much damage with the one in this article. (Though I have read that this point should be avoided by pregnant women.)

Ever had cramp? If you are not sure, or you cannot remember, then it's most likely you haven't!

I've certainly had cramp, toes, calf, and upper legs too. Thankfully not all at the same time! Just because we practice tai chi we are not immune from cramp, and I have noticed that cramp of the toes is a common visitor to some students.

I recall one particularly vicious bout of cramp, which attacked both legs simultaneously, during which I tried to relax with breath power, called on all the Gods for help, and interspersed it all with screams of "No, No, No, please No." Now according to my copy of 'The Sports Health Handbook', cramp can be treated by trying to relax the muscle and then massaging it, or better still, by over stretching the muscle fully. Faced with the almost overwhelming pain of sudden and uncoordinated contraction of all fibres in the muscle, both of these 'cures' are difficult, even with someone's help, and virtually impossible when on your own. The exact mechanism of cramp was not understood but it was thought that good nutrition could restore mineral deficiencies that might be a contributory factor. (magnesium)

Knowledge of which is little consolation at two in the morning as you lay in bed racked by immobilising pain; you're just never going to make it to the kitchen for that fruit and veg they recommend.

Sometimes we need the added power of belief to strengthen the remedy offered and here is mine.

Many years ago I went to a Yoga class, taught by a lady in her late eighties, who despite hip replacements and a frail body was able to demonstrate amazing ability and power. When she spoke I believed her, for she was the living proof of what she said. Occasional cramp would grip a student – mine was usually in my toes while trying to relax into 'child pose'- and she would say, "Press between the thumb and forefinger, it doesn't matter which hand."

No doubt this pressure point has a name, but, when cramp strikes, who cares what it's called as long as it works. You may well be familiar with this pressure point *(Hegu)* as it seems offered as help for various problems, so it would seem possible that its stimulation affects the whole body in some way.
Energy or pressure points are sensitive; if it hurts when you press then you've probably found it. It is located on the peak of the little mound that can be felt at the junction of thumb and fore finger. *See the diagram.*
You might ask me, "How long and how much pressure?"
I would ask you, "How bad is the cramp?"

In the absence of any better ideas, why not try it, I've had more than 90% success with it over the years. (If you have some secret for the other 10%, let us know.)

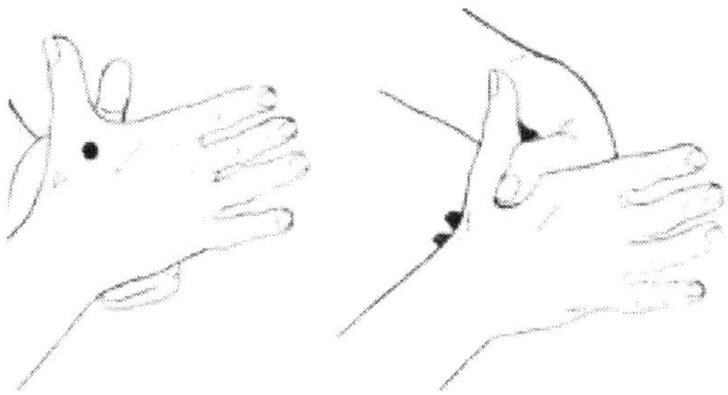

**

'Fear of making mistakes makes us tense,
but mistakes give us valuable information
in knowledge and skill, so,
do not fear them.'

**

23. Whatever you think

No doubt there'll be people who can't wait to read every word and enjoy it thoroughly, and there'll be those who will dismiss it at a glance and turn the page, and probably enjoy that too. Your choice.

> ***'Whatever you can do or dream you can, begin it. Boldness has genius, power and magic in it'***
>
> *Goethe.*

Whatever you think, I'm sure you can find more in life if you don't 'close doors' to insights that may come your way. Sometimes, when we close these doorways, they can remain closed to us forever, even if we do find them again. Isn't there an old saying, 'when opportunity knocks, open the door'? Or was it, 'opportunity knocks but once'?

Whatever you think, thoughts can create feelings, ... as they are in you now .... boredom, impatience, annoyance, intrigue, excitement, fascination ...., so, be careful what you think. It is all, of course deeper than we can ever know. There are also doorways to what seem complete opposites, like 'thinking destroys feelings', however, later you may see that they do complement each other in subtle but understandable ways; the rooms beyond the doors are interconnected.

Opposites are essential in our Universe ... try only breathing out!

Your life depends on both.

If you wish, let's go on a journey, a journey of mind into body; possibly we must use the thinking mind to start us off. We are going to try and create a physical feeling through a mental process.

Can you put your mind at the tip of your little finger? This is where a bit of thinking might help to start with. Ask the little finger tip how it feels, what is it like to be there, no where else, just the tip of the little finger. Try to sense what the little finger tip feels like. You should 'listen' with your non thinking mind, the feeling or awareness mind. Stay relaxed, especially shoulders and arms, you can try looking at the finger tips or try eyes closed. Something will work for you and be a willing partner in your experiment.

Can you manage this? Some will struggle and others will wonder what the fuss is about. That's life for you folks.

If you are struggling, don't give up, it could be one of your 'doors', so don't close it, you can do it.

Let us suppose a little success. In your mind move along each finger tip in turn, including the thumb. It doesn't matter how slow you go ... after all, you're not in a rush, are you? Try it a few times before we move further on our journey.

Now let's look at a special pressure point in the palm; Chinese name *Lao Gong*, English, *Palace of Toil*; when the fist is lightly closed the tip of the long finger, touches the Lao Gong point on your own palm. Lao Gong is on the pericardium meridian; but all we really need to know is that it has great value. Why not find it in your own palms, remember that most pressure points are in hollows.

Now armed with as much information as we need, we can proceed with our journey. We now put our minds into the finger nails, all of them, trying to sense, to feel, just what they might feel; be absorbed entirely by this process, this sensing. Be quiet and not distracted by anything else. You might find it easier to work on one hand first.

Now shift your mind to that *Lao Gong* point we looked at earlier; again, sense, feel, what it is like to be there, to be it, the *Lao Gong* point. Just do your best. Next, alternate between feeling fingernails and *Lao Gong*, as many times as you like and as slow as you like. Be patient, be focussed, you can open

this door.... and enter in. After several cycles you should become aware of something in the palm.
In the beginning we think and in the beginning our action seems physical, however, in time, from this purely mental process will come a physical manifestation; you may well 'feel' the *Lao Gong* point as a solid physical presence like you never have before. I hope you do, for then your door is open. Development of *Lao gong* is important for enhancing 'healing hands' in some therapies. More information is available via the internet ... but do you need it?
How can something happen when we do nothing? There are some Chinese sayings that give us a clue that in some ways this must be possible;

'To do less is to do more',
'do nothing, and everything is done'.

**

*What do **you** think,*
*because **that** is what **really** matters?*

**

"This Lao gong Light, this energy in the palms of our hands, holds incredible power. This is the power that moves mountains and creates worlds. This is the timeless, infinite energy of which we all are part. This is the Universal Life Force that flows without end through every being that lives, has ever lived, or ever will live across all time, space, realities and dimensions. It exists within and without. We cannot know it or understand it, we can only accept, it IS."
By my dear friend, Mya Gleny.

**

'Whatever you think, thoughts create feelings.'

**

***

24. Just some musings on 'energy'

Perhaps when reading this article your thinking mind is more active than your feeling senses. However, there may have been other times when you read some short sentence or phrase, or overheard one, and somehow a deep meaning or understanding became clear to you, yet the words alone did not seem to convey the same depth. You also discover it is not possible to repeat those words to another person and achieve the same result …. They don't 'see' what you 'saw'. Something connected at a deeper level than the thinking mind …. and, although you know it happened, you simply cannot explain it away. Perhaps it was your soul that understood it first.

Ever been part of a tai chi or similar activity group? Felt different in the group from being alone? Understood more while the teacher was with you, as though their very presence was in part responsible for teaching you?

Tai chi is an art that takes you into the moment itself... everything is in the present. Perhaps when you are in the

present moment and at the same time in a relaxed state which allows the chi (energy) to flow, then perhaps others in that same state can sense the same energy .... Because they too are connected to the very same space in time. A little like 'Namaste' for Yogis where they imply that when we are all in the place within where god resides, then we are as one..
Sometimes, even if we are 'believers', as you may well be if you are reading this, we can still experience a touch of scepticism at some of the therapies and claims to which we are exposed.

"**New!** As recommended by John Smith, author of Aliens Dug My Allotment and who once worked for NASA,.... The latest, Advanced Moon Therapy (AMT) ... You, yes, you, can receive the benefits of the mysterious energy of captured and stored white moonlight. Using a revolutionary yet mystic process, moonlight is metamorphed into Dark Side Light, (DSL) ... carrying away all your Earthbound fears and worries as it completes its cycle and is returned home to the dark side of the moon."

You tell a friend of this, convinced that there may be something in the advert.
"Yes," they reply, "... Lunacy!" Trouble is, the more times I read the advert .... I'm beginning to think it might even work!
Perhaps you'll think similarly of this article on energies and our various senses of them, but I don't mind. I am writing from my own experiences through my tai chi and other studies and know that many of you 'feel energy', and those that do not, probably can if they just 'looked'.
If nothing else it can create an interesting and rewarding exploration of who you might be during your days on earth, rather than be as the Japanese say *suisei-mushi*, born drunk and die still dreaming I believe it means.
We can exchange energy, borrow it or connect with it, some can see it and some can feel it, some want to know and others do not. What is the 'energy' I write of? Well I think it is usually

very subtle, probably is always there, needs patience, calm and often belief to open the door to feeling and can manifest in many ways but, even if the energy is identical, different people will describe the same sensation in quite different ways ... leading us to think there are many more energies. Description is often beyond us, as it is an experience that the thinking mind lacks ability to rationalise and we cannot articulate something we know exists but do not understand.

I knew a down to earth 40 year old carpet fitter from a village once who, during a closing down exercise saw his palms glow red, he had to look around the room to see where it might be coming from, he hardly dare speak of it, nor hope that he would see it again ... but he did.

I don't think I can see auras, but I once saw a lady's face change during a raja yoga meditation, four different faces plus her own; others also witnessed this event and their descriptions were similar. I also used to be able to see images of eyes while my own were closed, but on sharing this truly fascinating and absorbing activity with a friend he warned me, "stop doing it now," he said, "they are spirits coming to visit you, and if you are not careful one might stay!" I wished I had not listened, for I had never seen any eyes that looked harmful and after taking his advice have not seen any since. Beware closing a portal that you may never find again.

It is our perception that these things exist .... but where do they exist? Are they in the real material world or in some etheric non material dimension that we can by luck or will sometimes access? Perhaps these things are merely a fabrication of our own minds whereby they cannot fail to appear real, as happens during our dreams. Perhaps herein lies a clue as to why some can experience these things and others not. Some find it all just so easy; given the merest hint of what to do; all is revealed to them, whereas others struggle valiantly and find nothing .... ever.

Some amuse themselves with this energy, some use it for 'healing' or therapies. Wherever it comes from, wherever it goes, there is so often a beneficial effect from a therapy involving energies. Placebo it may be ... but who cares - if it works.

What is a placebo anyway ..... could it not be described as an energy for good itself? Is not belief a key to unlocking energy? They say that there is a measurable effect when a person prescribes a treatment in which they truly believe.... even if the treatment itself has no value; the value lies in the belief of the therapist; couldn't you say that this is an energy? Scientifically we are bound by the laws of physics, 'energy cannot be created or destroyed .... but it can be changed!' Light cannot be destroyed ... so where does it go then? But go it does, off into infinity at 186,000 miles per second.

Everything you do requires energy, of some description, known or not; thinking, dreaming, feeling, healing, breathing, living, all require some form of energy.

What else is out there we will fail to discover if we don't become explorers of our lives, our world.

In our tai chi classes we try and engage these energies as best we can.

I met up with a wise Russian recently while I was teaching tai chi in Greece. Himself a man of great ability I was honoured that he always came to my class; this is what my friend Sergei said, "You know the game for children where they seek a treasure and one who knows will call out, 'cold, warm, hot'? Our journey through life has these moments when we make some spiritual progress. We can't explain this to self but there is a sense that what we have experienced has taken us closer to what some might call God. For whatever that means to you, we merely wish to enjoy one step on the path together'." I'd like to think that he may have found one of those moments, when 'god' shouts "warmer", during my classes.

There are gateways you need to find, they exist in your body, like ming men, (gate of life), and in your mind.
You have to find them for yourself, but know this ...
they **are** there to be found. Then learn how to open them!

***

The following poem was written by my good friend, ***Sue Valentine,*** a talented artist and writer.

25. The Traveller's Song

Out on the hills, the road behind,
the path in front where it will wind,
the soft green ground, and sky of grey,
and peace to find along the way.

Out in the wind, a gusty kiss,
there is no better time than this,
unless a summer's soft embrace
is kinder to the travellers pace.

An open sky, and all around
such joy of spirit to be found,
and everywhere a new delight
to lift the soul to greater height.

The way is clear, and everything
is like a sip from some deep spring
out of the earth of long ago,
to cool the mind, and stroke the brow.

Some stay indoors, sit by the fire
and reading books they will aspire
to heath and moorland, hedge and trail
but surely not to much avail.

Put down your book, and come outside,
the road is free, the world is wide.
Come with me friend, and pass some time,
the path to tread, the hill to climb.

**

***As tai chi students we are also travellers,
take inspiration from her message.***

'Be the student to the end of days.'

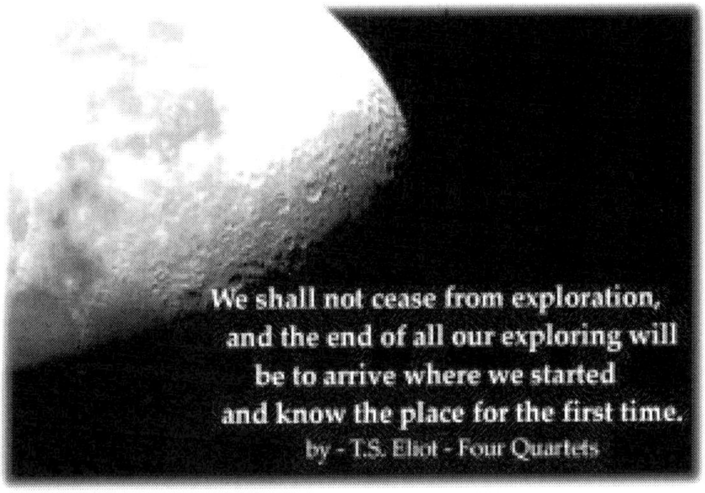

It's never the end.

Why put tai chi and aikido together?

Something tells me the founder of aikido would approve.
There are principles common to both arts and in each it is the application of principles and not mere technical choreography that is of the greatest importance. The arts are defined by how something is being done and not by what is done.
Though hamni or foot posture may be different, with a change in emphasis from heel to toe movements, the practitioner must regardless, only ever feel their body weight on their feet and not on hips or knees.
Though the practitioner's weight is a constant it should feel light to them and heavy to others. Balance and posture should always allow freedom of stepping.
If we approach - almost everything - with the mental attitude and body language required for meeting a nervous horse, then non judgement is ours and success will likely follow. Mental or body tension sends subliminal messages that will create fear, opposition or reaction.
Both arts require adapting body shape as required by events. While adapting body shape it should conform to that which feels natural, comfortable and provides optimum power.
Sneezing is a great analogy, your body will immediately adopt a natural posture that protects its integrity. About to sneeze? We never stand straight, we never keep the tea cup in our hands, we hold the steering wheel steady, we allow the body to adapt. Once the sneeze is over we tend to lose interest in natural body postures, we allow the mind to dictate, regardless of feeling.

So, constantly adapt, stay light in self, though heavy in body, and keep the mind non judgemental, allow feelings and body to inform the required action. This is the only rule your brain should make, after that it is down to the universal, the gods, spirits or chi/ki. In my opinion.

Part Two

AIKIDO WEAPONS

AND PRINCIPLES

A JOURNEY BEYOND CHOREOGRAPHY

By

RICHARD J. SMALL

Aikido weapons - engaging our minds beyond the technical.

Preferably you the reader will have some existing knowledge of aikido but none the less there is something in here of value for everyone. Just look for it. Through the medium of story and analogy, the purpose of this book is to offer you an opportunity to think, and to think in a way that creates an awareness leading more to sensory feeling. Though thinking destroys feeling, we often have to take that path in the beginning.

Be aware that intention and spirit are not quite the same and as for so called normal everyday thinking, that exists in your head alone. Belief is based on personal experience or at least your perception of it. Much is illusion, perhaps all.

Please don't take my word for any of it.

Always test ideas out for yourself.

I have expressed opinions based on my understanding at the time of writing, but in any case you should never follow blindly.

Make a point of learning
from the experience of your own practise.
Always be interested.

Also, and your teacher may have already told you, as eventually happens to all students in life,

'You are on your own in this journey.
You must therefore find your own way.'

Question in your own mind if what you read makes sense to you, for you are the map maker of your own world.

You are your own destiny -
if not, who the hell is?

Richard J Small

Dedicated to those who gave the gifts of learning and to those who might accept some of mine.

Mastering aikido

Mastering aikido is like finding some magical gem stone that emanates energy only in the hand of the true finder. The finder cannot see it or feel it but is aware of its existence and its effect on others. It is only uke (attacker), at the hands of the finder, that feels the power of the gem stone but they too cannot define nor explain its origins. Observers cannot see it either, except for the wonder on uke's face, that speaks of something magical and inexplicable having occurred.
To master aikido is to search for and find the invisible gem that exists not in some imagined foreign wilderness but hidden deep within each one of us. Go find.

I mean, how difficult can it be?

Part Two Contents.

Section 1. Philosophy and anecdotes.

Section 2. Technical and practical.

Section 3. Amusement only.

1. The Sculptor.

"Remove from your practice that which it isn't and, like the master sculptor, you will be left with that which it is."
"Like the master sculptor, you should be aware that there is always something better hidden within."

**

2. On teaching.

Teaching requires patience and humility as well as great skill. Teach others, don't just demonstrate how good you are. As we all learn in different ways, teach in different ways. Ideally the teacher will need ten times more knowledge than the student, as well as the skill to actually pass it on. Teaching is a great privilege and responsibility, for it can influence people's whole lives for good. True explorers don't keep secrets, they want to share their discoveries.

3. Aikido.... just what are the principles?

Pay attention to; - correct angle, distance, timing and attitude. Ensure; - weight underside, relaxation, concentration on one point (energy out), extension.

Nothing stands alone, everything is interconnected. However, we say the first principle is to escape the attack. . . which paradoxically we invite, then comes blending and connecting. In which order do they come? Shouldn't we have connected before the attack began? We take the attacker's balance. . . but do we, or do we lead them to an apparent place of safety, where they unknowingly give up their own balance.

There are the principles that relate to your interaction with the attacker during which you alter the circumstances of advantage to yourself.

Then there are principles that relate solely to your self, whether there is an attacker or not and which can and should be practised whether or not an attacker is present. Sound posture, balance and attitude. Correct connection throughout your own body and mind, your mind in the right place for the action. What you need from your mind is yet another deep paradox. How do you use your mind to do nothing, isn't using it actually doing something? How can you be 'out of your mind' yet still use it to extend Ki? Acting intuitively by body awareness may prove a better route than a technique based path but we must begin somewhere. I'm sure there are more questions I've as yet to discover. (A truly great teacher answers the questions that the student is never going to ask.)

There are principles for the body and those for the mind; is this something that can be understood but never explained? What do you think? It is what **you** think that matters, for it guides you in life. Become the observer of self as well as others. The true observer is not who you might think they are. Each of us can become two people, the observer and the observed, one is non judgemental the other is embroiled in it.

4. Doorways, gates, portals.

On our way, (Do), through life, we pass by many doorways of opportunity. Some we do not see, some we see but do not stop, some we try but they do not open, some open but we enter not therein, and some we enter through. Beyond those doorways we entered, there may be an enlightenment, a discovery, an experience, which we may or may not recognise for what it is, for 'seeing is not seeing'.

Sometimes we try to return to a doorway having realised its worth but now it may not open for us. We are indeed fortunate if we are awake to the opportunities that unfold before us, as you may find yourself now.

Why do we often ignore the offer of help from one who has gone before?

Many times we awake when the path has long ago passed by that doorway ... even in that there is a lesson to be discovered. The goal is the path itself and not as we usually think, the destination, for there isn't one, we only think there is.

'Tomorrow does not exist, it never has!'

Our path is blessed if it travels through time in Ai Ki (harmony of spirit). Keep your eyes on the path and what is on it. Eyes looking far into the distance mean none on the path. Beware that the fog of thinking can obscure the doorways. Consider the paradox of, not thinking and yet all will be revealed.

Keep the mind moving, seek change.

Thought is not required, what is required is inspiration and intuition. Both of these will arrive uninvited when the thinking mind is quiet.

'Calm is always the key'.

***

5. An interview with the author, July 2017

Q. What inspired you to teach aiki jo (short wooden staff)?

Training with weapons needs no mats, it is something you can practise alone or with a partner, you can practise in street clothes and footwear, anywhere you go, the forest, the beach, your home or garden - you can pick up any stick, broom handle, hoe, umbrella, walking stick, even a twig and enjoy your connection with the spirit of aikido. As a teacher moving to the area alone, it was an art that lent itself to teaching beginners who had neither equipment nor experience.

It is also an art within the reach of almost any person, regardless of their age and ability.

Q. What are the aims of martial arts?

Qualities imbued in martial arts practice.
Perception; awareness; confidence; patience; friendship; communication; adaptability; resilience; loyalty; reflection; humility; perspective; compassion; honesty; empathy; discipline, (both external and self); humour; co-ordination, (of mind and body); flexibility; intuition.

These are transferable skills
that will always serve you well in life.
They are freely yours for the having.

Aiki Jo can also be used as an exercise system, training aspects of self defence, developing health defence, improving confidence, body awareness, co-ordination, social and self awareness, balance and power, even engaging in a pathway to moving meditation and finding the path on which your spirit walks.

Weapons encourage your spirit energy to extend beyond self.

Q. What plans do you have for the future?

I started a martial art when I was in my twenties, probably for much the same reason as anyone else. I sought a security from the imagined confrontations that beset the minds of youths.

Martial arts are a great reality check for the Ego. You suddenly discover that the art you have taken up to defend yourself is full of people much more capable than you. You try harder to catch up, to improve fitness, co-ordination and technical skills. Often, it is many years before the spiritual side of the art becomes apparent. The mind/body/spirit connection makes you more calm, centred, and peaceful; And yes, more powerful. Do not confuse strength with power. When you understand, 'Do nothing and everything is done,' then you have arrived at the gateway you seek. After more than forty years of training, I plan to keep looking and try and make what I understand, possible through my actions. Still a long way to go – but the journey remains ever more important than the destination. In a gentle way I am now exploring combat jujitsu as a beginner. . . emphasis on gently!

***

6. Remembering my teacher's lesson

A recollection from 1998 and my teacher's lesson. They were often carried out with short stories –
"the path there is and many seek it, the map there is and many hold it. As we progress, more of the map becomes clear. Sometimes a tree (a problem) will bar our way. If we detour then, we must remember why we did so, for if the tree is later removed, we must return to the old path.

> ***The detour was not the true path,***
> ***merely a convenience of the time.***

Eventually we will not seek the path nor will we ever know that we are on it, for then, we will *be* the path."

***

7. Of Aikido and of leaves in Kefalonia.

(An analogy with aikido. . . but you're going to have to find meanings for yourself!)

Early one fine summer's morning, when an Ionian Sun had just risen above the skyline of Mount Aenos and yet already bathed the garden in a fiery light, the student selected one of the brooms by the back door and headed left to a nearby leaf strewn path. Lesson one, be careful what you choose; that refers to both broom and path!

He knew there were lessons to be had in sweeping the path; lessons often more profound than we can imagine; perhaps one would show itself this day.

There are, of course, many paths, each with its own teaching; the one shown in the photo is not the path he chose to sweep. Why might you think that it was? ***Seeing is not seeing*** and we are beset by illusion and inference in life, sometimes we foolishly 'assume'. Yet often the correct answer will be an opposite of that which we at first thought. Think on this, for it is a valuable principle to use in life.

The uneven surface of the grey, crazy paved stones seemed to trap the fallen eucalyptus leaves that covered the path. The brush he had inadvertently and unquestioningly chosen was a stiff bristled synthetic affair and he at first blamed it for its failings, indeed he blamed it for all failings, thinking that a wider, softer one would be much more effective. Was this the lesson? No, it seemed not, there surely must be more. Keeping the brush he had chosen but changing the direction of sweep soon had the reluctant leaves shifted from their erstwhile homes.

Could this be the lesson. . . changing direction?
It was certainly one of sorts but surely he must look further, deeper. Perhaps using the brush was just practice for the Jo. Could it be that simple?
He began to move leaves from right to left so that he could more easily sweep a whole line of them over the edge into the oblivion that lay beyond the formalised garden. This wasn't a punishment for the leaves; they were going to be happier where he sent them. Many went willingly. His plan functioned reasonably well and the majority were easily brushed away and dismissed from the perceived battlefield. It however left a few tenacious, conflict hardened beasts that denied his every move. Even on flat stones the elongated Eucalyptus leaves clung like limpets. The harder he brushed the more they resisted, looking up mockingly at his efforts, laughing, as if they knew all the secrets and they could clearly see that he did not. The more strength he added to the brush the closer it came to failing in itself, and he with it.
He paused, relaxed a little and instead tried the lightest touch with the brush and, there in the capitulating tumbling leaves, lay the answer. Use correct technique and never add power; concern yourself only with disrupting the leaves' stability, take their balance and only engage in a direction which will prove useful. Then the leaves will cease to become opponents but become partners on the path. No energy was added to the weight of the leaf by pressing, instead the energy ran parallel to the ground and once the leaf was ungrounded it was at the brush's mercy . . . and none was given !

Another day arrived; another brush was chosen and before him, the same path, now fresh strewn with wind blown debris from the generous Eucalyptus that forever shared its leaves with the earth. The brush, new to him yet perhaps old to others, was softer. "This is much better," the student thought satisfyingly, "much better. . . no need for great pressure, this soft brush is working well." Each piece of stone was swept, each piece of stone was new, and each sweep of the brush was new. Perfection was sought with every single action as if it was unique and all that existed; smooth, flowing, efficient and successful; then, on to the next stone and the process repeated in a manner as if it were again the first time.

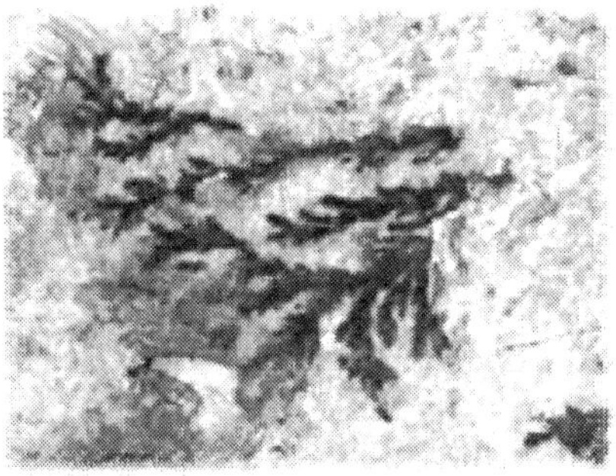

Suddenly a gift appeared before his eyes, there in the stones so carelessly swept before, he saw the signs of ancient life. . . fossilised plants and perhaps a promise of more to find. Now each stone was brushed more carefully, the student's awareness raised to what the moving leaves might uncover. What joy, what discovery might be behind every leaf on the path. . . the destination became the path itself. The routine of sweeping a path became a series of profound lessons. Brush, leaves, stones, the path and the student himself, all took on new meaning.

When someone asks you to sweep their path, accept it as a gift and think on what I have written, for nothing will ever be as you think it is. Much, if not all of your world, is illusion, as this too may be.

***

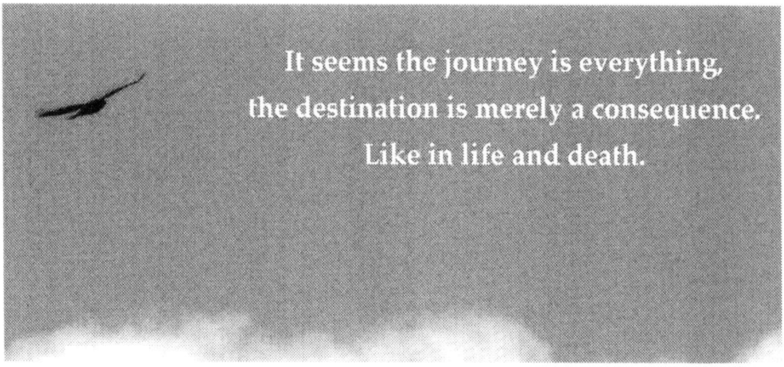

8. Sweeping the temple floor.

In many an Aiki Dojo across the world, it is not an uncommon day break practice to sweep the surrounding yards and pathways. Why is it done? For the pride in your Dojo? To keep visitors feet clean for the tatami? So that the Sensei can exert power over you? Because the Sensei had years of path sweeping under his belt too?

Let us consider our reasons. The early morning cleansing sweep is no different as dawn rises at Sensei Tony Sargeant's Koriana Dojo on Kefalonia. (*Now closed*) The change is not just for the path surface but for the sweeper; perhaps the sweeper becomes the swept.

Rising before 6.00am, students sweep the paths and courtyards of the Koriana Dojo in the warm dawn air; as they sweep pristinely onwards, nature acts as nature does and once more decorates the ground with fallen leaves and bougainvillea flowers behind them. What change there? ...the ground itself is still the same. . .only the leaves are new. The circle is endless. Perhaps in this we have a clue.

We may also, through our endeavours, recognise that which we can change and that which we cannot; another clue as to purpose.

So, why do we do it? Firstly, it is expected of you. There may be a penalty to pay should you arrive late. (Ah, is this another

lesson here?) We learn to obey, both the Sensei and the rules but we also learn to share and to care. We work in harmony with others, avoiding sweeping our collected debris and troubles on to another's space. Blending our efforts in harmony we help those who struggle with the task and we accept help from those who give. (Any lessons there?)
You sweep for the sake of others, that their trials and sufferings as they may be, are not worsened by your own omissions or lack of effort. You let no one down; a humble and humbling task has become an honourable achievement; a sense of this flows within you, you are a small step further down the path of Aiki, a small step, a small victory.

Perhaps the 'why' and the 'how' of the matter are inextricably entwined.

Is the purpose only to have a clean path? No, it surely is not, for that is a destination that may never be reached. As ever, the path is the goal itself, the path you walk is your destination.
How should you sweep? Well that is up to you to discover. **What** should you think? That too is up to you, for it is your own individual path to follow. . . and your path to sweep. (An old proverb says, 'he who is carried to the temple gates will never know how far it was.') {*Repeated again because of its value.*}
I share with you here my current and no doubt transient understanding which I encountered while sweeping such a path.
<u>Time</u> – it is always so hard to find the time, so we have to make the time, and the Dojo at dawn is when you make the time to sweep the path.
<u>Sensitivity</u> – applying the pressure and in a way that the flimsy dojo brush will not bend or break. (Believe me, they do, as someone I know quite well has broken three already!)
<u>Patience</u> – how to move the tiny leaves that grip the earth like a hundred kilo 9th Dan and yet simultaneously how to control

the little round seeds that roll and scatter in all directions
Control – how to hold the brush and explore tsuki or gedan gaeshi; a chance to explore the inner connections of both body and mind in a peace of your own making; a chance to repeat the movement a thousand times yet with each movement of the brush, we engage the beginner's mind.
Beginner's mind – the beginner's mind is ever in the 'now'. Each new sweep of the brush is a 'now' moment in which all is new yet all is changing. No preconceptions about the next sweep, no memories of the last one. . . unless you broke the brush. Think on this next time you practice in aiki.
Inner calm – as you begin to sweep, the thinking mind is active yet soon transforms to the intuitive realm as the simplicity of your task leads you to a calmer state of mind.
Attacker or attacked? perhaps the path is uke to your nage. . . or perhaps it is nage to your uke . . . or is it neither . . and you are one. . .you decide.

So many lessons there are on the path,
be attentive and they may show themselves.

9. A principle that weapon's practice supports.

Regardless of style, how often will you have heard the advice, 'extend', whether it be to extend ki or merely to reach out physically? When you extend ki there will always be an unintentional and often unrealised slight physical extension. It is better to think of it in an energy way rather than extending only physically, for that can lead to tightening of muscles and locking of one's own joints.

If you observe any of the great masters their 'extension' is evident, it is clearly visible. Old film of O-Sensei shows his extension both energetically and physically. So let us presume this is an important part of the art we follow.

How do you use your Aiki weapons? Do you extend your mind into the weapons? Do you reach out, keeping joints relaxed but open? Do you maintain good connection, not only between you and the Jo but with your arms and the rest of your body? Are you relaxed and yet focussed (concentrated) in your movements? Is the grip you have, relaxed, connected and effective? Do you keep the Jo (weapon) in harmony with your body? Do you change body posture in order to create a better grip?

Explore an idea; Try any weapons move you know. . . preferably very slowly, and consider the relationship with yourself and the Jo at all times during the move.

Is your own action causing your joints to be stressed? A common example is in high Tsuki (thrust), if the hand is too far away from your body there is a tendency for the fingers to be wrenched open ... aikido isn't meant to inflict damage to your own body. Hands should always be able to retain a relaxed grip; this allows the shoulders to relax too. If it doesn't feel right then it probably isn't right. Using the mind to extend Ki does not mean that any of your joints are locked nor your muscles tight. . . a controlled relaxation is the result. In the high tsuki mentioned earlier, the arm may be bent but there is a sense of opening and reaching out which gives it its power. . . it is truly connected and at one with the whole body. Extending Ki is an essence in weapons work and therefore can develop that principle into a habit that is available to you in all your aikido. Feet, knees, hips, shoulders, elbows, hands and jo - all in harmony with each other. This might sound strange to you, but each elbow should 'feel' the same as the other, regardless of differing postures.

Sergei Stoliarov and Mark Allcock, Kefalonia

10. Ki, extension and relaxation equals power.

Ki . . . Imagination. . . belief gives birth to power . . . the energy can become a reality.
Extension with relaxation enables the body to unite as a whole, leading to power.
The power is in the joints – in the space between them. Just like the space in a wall is the gateway to another place. If you are familiar with the 'unbendable arm exercise' you will recognise this. The space between contains opposites which work in harmony to create a whole. Believing in expanding your aura can lead to a physical expression of expansion by your body.
When relaxing you should feel a quiet, calm expansion in the joints, the mind is drawn to outside of the body rather than within and the sensation of weight on the body becomes lifted as the feeling of having joints disappears.

"In nothingness, there is everything".

***

11. Concern for teaching. . . my question answered.

"We never know what we give until it's been given, and then we may be the last to know if it did arrive in the way we thought it should."

Tony Sargeant Sensei 6th dan aikikai

***

12. Fear is the crossing place.

Find the balance between the defeat of your mistakes and the inflation of your successes.
The middle way is calm and relaxed.

Fear of making mistakes creates a tension that prevents you crossing to a better place.

Don't let thoughts take away feelings,
for it is they that might guide you all the better.

**

13. Why do we bow to O-Sensei ?

These are entirely my own views, based upon the teachings of others and my own experience. It's an amalgamation of eastern and western culture but which retains value for self and respect for others.

Bowing is a mark of respect in many cultures, so it follows that respect is primary. You might add other feelings too, gratitude or admiration for a start. Perhaps you only bow out of habit, because everyone else in the class does. It becomes just another thing you carry out before warm ups and the 'proper' aikido that you signed up to do. Perhaps you bow mindlessly, thoughtlessly, without feeling. Perhaps your bow is meaningful but travels only one way . . . 'what can O-Sensei do for me?'

I am of the opinion that to gain the most from your practice you are best bowing consciously, perhaps with a sense of both giving and of receiving. Strange as it may seem, the act of kindness and its effects, confer more power upon you than not. So in a way, kindness is unselfishly selfish.

Respect the mat and the dojo, respect your teacher and partner and respect is returned. This is a good lesson for everyday life and in part this too is one of the great benefits of training in the art.

Sometimes students clap their hands during the bowing sequence. It might well be said that you should only clap if there is a kamiza present. (The little wooden house where it is imagined the spirits dwell.) The clapping is supposedly to request that the spirits join you and help you in your quest. Once again that seems a one way street of, 'what's in it for me?'

There may be more than one reason for placing the hands together in 'prayer' position. Connecting hands in such a way connects left side of body with right side, making you naturally whole. It connects two major pressure points (nerve centres) in the palms together, one side being Yin and the other yang. It creates a balance of opposites with harmony.

I read recently that the first of two claps is to connect outwardly, to send out your spirit to connect with the universal and that the second clap is inviting the universal to come and join with you. You can try this for yourself, I'd almost make a bet that you will find it very difficult to experience either the out or the in whilst making the clap. It is easier when your mind is quiet and the body not active.

Whatever you chose to do and for whatever reason, you will still find it beneficial to have a purpose of good intent and to engage with it meaningfully. Keep vigilant for new learning.

In my own weapons practice, I mentally offer my Jo to the image of O-Sensei as a gift. I then imagine that he offers it back, saying, 'no, you take it back and practise well with it.' It is often what we think or believe what influences the outcome and I found that a deeper understanding of giving and receiving is achieved.

There is more to Aikido than technique!

If you ever think you have arrived,
then you have lost the path.

Ken tai jo in Cambridge

14. Let wisdom be the hero for the day.

My soul didn't ask me to write this, it demanded it of me. The trouble is the language of the soul doesn't translate very well into English and there are some concepts that find no words in our language. However, I shall do my best, which is probably what you do too... or at least that's what we often say we do.
Poor old O-Sensei, he had such a noble dream to reconcile the world in peace through aikido. It might just be possible if we all tried harder for that goal. I am minded of a story about two birds discussing snow and its weight. One said, "Snow is so light, it weighs nothing, why, I have seen it lifted in the wind." The other replied, "I think not friend, for I once watched snow landing on a mighty tree branch, snow flake after snow flake and the branch held strong . . . until just one more tiny snowflake landed and that branch was felled. . . just one more that's all."

The moral being perhaps that in life situations, we can be that tiny thing that finally tips the balance.

But I digress, the soul wants me to write of other things; to question why we might do aikido, what qualities do we seek, if at all, what teachers we might follow, who do we think should be practising aikido or not, more importantly; who or what do we aspire to, who to emulate, who to cast aside. Are they not all snowflakes? If none of this means anything to your own soul don't read any more, go and do something that you think is more important. It's your soul that matters and not the calculating, time constrained egoistic left side of your brain; you know the side that just looked at how many more lines there are to read, or the clock, or thought about a snack, or what's on TV.

It's the side of the brain that will let you down one day when it decides it doesn't know the answer... an answer that your soul knew from birth but you would not listen.

When we are young, lots of not so old people actually look really old to us and we foolishly look down on them, seeing them as less able or defective in some way that we of course are not. I learned a lesson many years ago for which I remain grateful. I had not been practising aikido that long but had risen to the dizzy heights of yellow belt. My teacher at the time, Sensei Aubrey Smith, had organised a workshop with a visiting teacher at our small dojo in Wellingbrough. I sat on a chair in the dojo along with another yellow belt, I think his name was Mick, a swimming instructor he was. We were waiting for a few more to turn up when this seemingly short and elderly chap came in and put a briefcase down on a chair before leaving the room again. Mick and I looked at each other, we were amazed that this little old chap (as we saw him from our twenty year old eyes) was going to attempt aikido. Didn't he realise it was a martial art and required youth and strength to perform. . . why, he was just wasting his time. Our Sensei entered and we lined up ready for the start; the visiting teacher entered and we were totally gob-smacked that it was the old chap we had written off before. He was a second Dan at the time and we know of him now as 8th Dan Sensei Pat Stratford. I was to meet Sensei Pat again when we travelled to his club in Coventry, where he hosted a course with Sensei Andre Noquet of France . . . another old man, (from our twenty year old eyes). Please realise that I write with affection and respect for these masters, past and present. I may not remember the techniques but I remember the men and the lessons I learned and I have gratitude for their unstinting devotion to the art and to the efforts they made to share it with others.

I also recall an elderly man who trained with us in Cambridge; it was annoying if I found that he was my partner because I couldn't throw him about and inflict my 'aikido' on him like with a younger 'proper' uke. How sad that we can practice an art about which we often understand nothing. It shouldn't have mattered about his age, it is not up to uke to develop our aikido but it is up to us; another valuable lesson from the 'has-beens' as we so foolishly think them.

O-Sensei was an old man,
why don't we discount him too,
or perhaps you have.

There are a few of these older chaps about (I'm one myself now!) and so often they have little publicity and fewer students, a handful at most. Many students want a dynamic teacher, a Bruce Lee type, not someone who looks like they live in an old people's home. They choose a teacher that fits their mind set and what they think they want from aikido; that too will change them with the lengthening years . . . if they keep going that is, for many will abandon the art when it no longer suits their ageing body. The art will never abandon us, it is we who are guilty of that deed. The older teacher probably has the answers to which the younger student hasn't even discovered the questions.

Whatever we do in life, much of it will have depended on the help of others. . . you'd be dead now if your parents hadn't fed and looked after you, you don't make your own clothes you probably don't gather your own food, you wouldn't be reading this if someone hadn't taken the time and trouble, to teach, to help and guide you. You think you did it all yourself? Then you suffer from another problem that martial arts should help you with. . . ego, let's make that **Ego**. O-Sensei wrote about taking the sword and cutting down the enemy. And where did he suggest we would meet this enemy? Inside, of course. What form did O-Sensei suggest this enemy would take? I'm not sure that he extrapolated on his suggestion but I would hazard a guess that it wasn't anything on the following list; loyalty, honour, integrity, gratitude, patience, endurance, tenacity, compassion, generosity, understanding, harmony, spirit, in fact harmony of spirit through our endeavours.

I nearly wrote some more there, but have deleted it as I realised it was not my soul but my thinking brain that wanted to say it and there is no place here for such thoughts.
I will close by thanking all my teachers whoever they were or are, in life or in death, some gem of wisdom has stayed with me from each and every one, I am grateful for all the efforts they made in the search of their art and their willingness to share it freely.

Let wisdom be the hero for the day.

***

15. Remembering and learning

We forget much, even some of the really important things, but because we still actively study the art, we come across new learning. Someone opens the gateway to what was hitherto hidden from view ... perhaps it is even our own gate that we kept closed until then. Armed with our new learning, old memories are triggered and we see the similarities for the first time. We have joined two more pieces of the great puzzle. Only by more study will we discover the other pieces, so, never close your mind to what might be. Discovery brings with it a new level of joy and excitement.

Never give up the search

***

16. What's wrong with Aikido if you want it as street style self defence.

What's good about it if you want a spiritual path that aids your well being.

No mats - can't do - why not ... want to throw
Examine attitude ... winning - it's the attitude that is wrong - beware ego - shame
During half the class some are only learning to be useless.

No old people - no children - creates a false reality.

I'm sure, just like I have, you have considered the stylised attacks we so often see in aikido training. You will probably have also noted that the typical street attack uses none of these . Most street attacks will involve an arm reaching out, either to grab or to range-find or will involve a direct swinging punch to the side of the head. Even primitive man was aware of the effects of a blow to almost any area on the side of the human head.
Perhaps our aikido isn't preparing us for these attacks but developing transferable skills. Even so, the half hearted, probably won't hit you anyway, pre telegraphed and slow strikes that end with a dead stop and a long wait for the defensive move to occur might still provide useful training for nage. I suggest that it is counter productive training for uke. They are learning to telegraph moves, overbalance themselves, lose awareness, expect to fall over and expect to lose. Sometimes you see the uke prepare for the ukemi before nage has effected the technique. This is a wonderful example of blending and compliance but I suspect it is short changing the student for half of his training session . . . the half in which he is uke.
I think the attacker should be placed by nage in a position where they realise they cannot win and that they will arrive at that point not knowing how it happened. Because what they do not know, they cannot counter. If nage blends with, then 'attacks' their opponent or partner, then that attack will be felt. Something more subtle exists ... it is aikido ... what are we doing ?

***

17. What's your opinion on relaxation in Aikido?

I'd like to share some thoughts and learn from those that might offer their own. I'll say a little more on interpreting the term relaxation later but, regardless of its manifestation.

'Relaxation can save your life;
stress and panic can take it.'

For example:-
Worry ... is paying a price that may never be asked.
Swimming, float when caught in a rip tide.
Confined space... trapped...a relaxed body is smaller.
Boxing.... No endurance without relaxation, no speed without it either.
Car crash... not suggesting you should drink and drive, but drunks nearly always walk away.
Breakfalls... relaxed, don't hold breath. Tension may be injurious.
Note how all the above bear a direct relationship to the all important point of contact. How you interact with it determines the success or not of the outcome. Does that not apply to our aikido?

Tension, too much want and resistance, are
surely enemies of good aikido.

Success comes from, not adding, but in giving something up, like a great sculptor removing the worthless to reveal the perfection beneath.
Even intention can create tension. The initiation of intent encourages the hidden muscles in your body to cooperate with that intent and subtly engages them. This tension is visible to highly experienced martial artists even though the person they observe may not be aware of it at all. This

intention effect can be experienced in most if not all of Ki exercises. The relaxation we really want is a relaxed connectedness, no slack in joints and nothing more to connect, before moving.
So, if you are going to have intention at all, let it be the to connect the whole body without tension and avoiding any single directional approach.
This brings us on to compliance or complicity in practise. How can you practise your art if the attacker goes along with every thing you do – even if your 'technique' was completely incorrect.
If you apply a lock with force, are you not then becoming the attacker and therefore vulnerable to the skilled aikido practitioner. But of course they are not allowed to use it, because it is not their turn.
Should not the attack be as meaningful as a real one within the sensible limits of practise and the receiver lead the attack without force to a place where the attacker's power and balance are so weak that they succumb to the 'technique' without argument or even an understanding of how it happened. Using force gives the other person information on power and direction. The only reason you can feel your own power is because it is coming back to you, what comes back to you can be used by others against you.
If you meet force with force then usually the strongest wins. As we know, this is not the principle we adopt in aikido, in fact we might advertise the art as one in which a small person can use the power of a larger more powerful adversary against them. At times this appears laughable but with real skill, probably more than most of us will ever find, it must be possible.
So, what do you think about complicity in practise, where the attacker ends up having the essential sensitivity and relaxation that should be the prerogative of the receiver?

The man we purport to follow
yet mostly seem to ignore.

Huw Collingbourne founder of Hartland Aikido in Devon says,

"My own view is that if you are true to the essence of aikido you must both take away the strength *and* (using balance and blending) make the technique work. 'Softness' is no excuse for ineffective technique. The technique must *always* work, no matter how soft your style may be. If your technique fails you must go away and re-think it, not (a) ask the uke to behave differently (as far as I am concerned the uke is always right and should never be blamed for a failed technique) or (b) make it work by adding in strength. It is the constant search for effectiveness without force that makes aikido a continuing challenge even for people like us who've been doing it most of our adult lives."

And from *'Takemusu Aikido' A Martial Artist's Journey of Discovery in Aikido.* *By Tony Sargeant – 6th Dan Aikikai*

'I felt full of confidence and ready to show Sensei just how good I was and I was certain the compliments would come in abundance the moment he first used me as Uke. This was far removed from what actually happened. Saito Sensei was so delighted once he heard a person had come all the way from England just to train with him that I was given the best position in front of his teaching. After only one day I was in front on the mat holding his wrist and I knew I had him. I was grounded and his soft squidgy wrists seemed completely mine, I squeezed just that bit more and he very slightly staggered. I knew my ten years of hard training was paying off. The next second I was thrown as if I were a piece of scrunched up cigarette paper and as I looked up from the ground, wondering what had happened, Saito Sensei spoke to the class of Auckland University students with these words: *"Tony is the strongest man on this Tatami (mat). . . I feel sorry for him; if he does not lose his strength he will never find O-Sensei's aikido".* From the moment he said "Tony is the strongest man on this mat' to "if he does not lose his strength" I went from bathing in great glory to feeling the size of a mouse.'

Such students go on to become true masters of the art.
A title they readily deny and who too few will follow.

***

18. A great paradox to success .... I think.

Seeing what you desire in the pool of water, you reach in to make it yours. But when you pull it out it is no longer what you saw. Seeing and perspective can be illusions.

What you search for you must try hard to find, but in its finding, what you looked for will disappear. It will be there but you won't know it as the thing you first sought.

Though you must try hard to find, beware of trying so hard that the trying overshadows the discovery that may come from a different way, a smarter trying.

What you look for may arrive when you look in the opposite direction and are able to see it for the first time. If this reads a bit weird, I'm not surprised, yet I am happy with my understanding so far of this paradox.

The more you think, the harder will be the discovery but one day in some unthinking moment, the answer will be yours.

A poor diet is not good for our health.

Just by knowing the words, can we call this true 'awareness'? Awareness of words alone cannot reach the depth of knowing which is truly worth seeking.

I once heard an interesting analogy about warehouses; if you want to build a home, then you visit the warehouse for your bricks and timbers. Now, what if the only materials collected are damaged. **'Sorry, we only have twisted timbers, some with woodworm, and crumbly broken bricks'.** What sort of home can you build with them?

Now, our subconscious is our own warehouse from which we take the materials to build our 'home' - the place in which the inner you lives.

Therefore be careful what you store in your warehouse, for upon this will depend the sort of 'home' in which you inhabit this earth.

So, for aikido. or any other art, put only the best materials into your warehouse, seek quality foundations - for they are your future; gather and build carefully with attention to detail, do not rush, build yourself a lovely home - for it is you and you alone that lives in it - until it falls down or there's a power failure!

Build well and you might live happier and longer.

***

19. Are you right in what you do?

Are you confident that you know what you are doing?

Is what you are doing what you actually thought it was or would be?

After more than 40 years practising the art, I am now hitting a confused patch. Not that what I have done didn't seem to work at one time but I wonder now if it was real ai ki do. Was it really a harmony of spirit that I had? Did I inflict my aikido on others? Did I use my spirit enough? Did I co-ordinate my whole body and mind enough? Was my desire to win too much? Should I have been more sensitive to the physical attack and more empathetic with the mind of the attacker? Should I even have considered it an attack and not a 'gift'. . . does this in itself contravene the spiritual ethic of aikido? I am no longer sure about these things but continue to look forward to finding out.

We often tell others, 'I do aikido', but do we really? What is real aikido, what was O-Sensei's discovery all about?

'The journey is everything and for each of us
there is only one destination;
it's how we make our way there that matters.'

Is the path itself the destination?
Even O-Sensei would tell you that he had yet to arrive at a destination where all was known.

The path is the destination.

***

The late Tim Buswell Sensei with tachi dori

***

If your heart is large enough to envelop your adversaries, you can see right through them and avoid their attacks. And once you envelop them, you will be able to guide them along the path indicated to you by heaven and earth.

***

20. Takemusu – the truce in war.

No doubt like many oriental words, the meaning of '**takemusu**' is liable to interpretation and the singularity of the word itself belies the volume of meaning it carries. In fact to those who know the kanji,

It is debatable if the word 'musu' is correct, however, semantics and Chinese origins to pronunciation aside, this is what O-Sensei called it. That alone should be good enough for us if we are willing to understand what he was prepared to share.

The heart of it is, Takemusu relates to the spontaneous creation of technique during a moment of harmonisation between attacker and defender. (Possibly even the use of the word defender may be too strong. The act during the takemusu moment is natural, peaceful, effortless yet unstoppable, to use the word 'defend' creates an impression of more overt effort and an imposing action.) We know by now that words are an imperfect tool and that only the foolish will take them at face value.

'The wise hear one word,
but understand two,'

- An old saying of some merit.

Let us take the analogy of war. One country looks at another with which it has grievance or designs and if it thinks it has the power to overcome that country it might attack using its military force. But supposing the attacked country has skills, culture, weaponry or whatever, that stops the attacker's advance. There is a moment when the attacking country realises their mistake and seeks a truce. At this point two conflicting views come together as one view – that of the truce itself. Two opposing forces temporarily live together in harmony and terms are settled in favour of the country which was attacked. Remember the attackers have realised their efforts are to no avail, they have no hope of succeeding. If the country which was attacked negotiates a peaceful settlement without causing great suffering to the would-be assailants then the attacker can accept defeat. Should the winning side impose draconian reparations upon the loser then they have become the attacker and as history has always shown a vengeful continuation of repeated wars is the result.

I think that the truce in war, with all its realisations during a short period of non confrontation, is much like the Takemusu moment. It must carry honourable principles in order to have a lasting legacy.

Further to this, I think takemusu is more than just a moment in time. It is a moment in time that embodies the trained principles of your aikido and the spirit that was invoked by our founder.

In the execution (unfortunate word) of our aikido, mind must connect with body and yet being 'in the body' is more powerful than 'being in the mind'. We need to be balanced or our own consciousness is restricted, our 'inner' must be in accord with our 'outer' if our power is to manifest itself. In the takemusu moment, do not exert yourself in a way that you feel your own power, because if you can, then you are becoming the attacker again.

Your attacker must not be able to understand your power, only know it exists.

The attacker (or Uke, partner etc in aikido training) should reach a point where they realise it is futile to resist, in fact there is no desire to resist as no direct force is felt. With their balance taken they are lost and will fall. It is unnecessary to add force to their fall . . . it is their turn next, just like in the history of wars. So it is not just down to correct technique but the timing, manner and judgemental free attitude of the aikidoka that allows the takemusu event to be successful . . . physically and spiritually. It is almost an act of kindness in the face of the enemy, and

'one cannot defend oneself against kindness.'

On a personal note here, I have never been one of those brave ukes, but when my teacher threw me in Koshi nage I was happy to go with it. There was no force applied that I could resist and therefore to flow over the hips and to the mat seemed like the most desirable direction to go. Compare with some people who grab your arms and physically try and wrench you over, using an arm to flip your legs and perhaps giving a quick hip lift to ensure maximum effect. Once you feel the physical or known power of the thrower then you can resist, because you understand what they are doing, you know how to stop them. And the war continues. This is not aikido and certainly is missing the magic of takemusu which is effortless, kindly and superbly effective.

The truce leads to a peace with honour.

***

21. O-Sensei's poems, what do they mean to you?

I've chosen one verse from many; can it have meaning for you, a meaning that possibly is only for you. It is often the way, for to each of us the very same something can appear quite different.

"Standing amidst heaven and earth
connected to all things with ki
my mind is set
on the path of echoing all things."

Morihei Ueshiba

My interpretation is firstly that of an awareness that it is Earth that holds me up, (if, in your mind, you stand not on the earth but let the earth push upwards, strangely you will feel lighter) and an indefinable concept of some on high celestial heaven, essentially a place in your mind that is above you. (Might just be a concept created from extending consciousness beyond self and manifesting a sense of connection with the top of your head, the crown chakra or celestial gate).

Much of this 'mind work' is about creating mechanisms that in turn allow you to experience feelings that would otherwise be difficult to ever find.

O-Sensei suggests **'standing amidst'**, so we can imagine heaven and earth as two separate entities and place ourselves between them. We then become the connection and the bridge between heaven and earth. (You may feel a slight and involuntary elongation in your spine when you do this. Opening spaces within the body is a way of becoming one with the spaces in the universe – for they are the same).

O-Sensei continues; **'connecting with Ki'**: imagine now your own consciousness, aura, Ki, life force, what ever you wish to call it, expanding in all directions, reaching out and as it does

so touching the energies of everything around you . . . and as far out into the cosmos as you like, for your imagination is boundless.
The **'echo of all things'** is merely your awareness that your own 'Ki' has touched and recognised the oneness in all it touches.

Well, for what it's worth, this is my interpretation at my current level of understanding. Perhaps if O-Sensei was here and I could understand him he might say, 'total cobblers' or perhaps 'not bad but keep looking'.

We will never know . . . or will we?

***

22. Do you want to know a Secret?

The founder is known as the great teacher, but I ask you, 'Do you know anyone, living or dead that reached the same level as O-Sensei? So, if he was the great teacher, why, despite commitment, techniques and principles, couldn't anyone else reach his level?
What he knew, at an esoteric level, he could not teach. Paradoxically it may have been the very mastery of his art itself that prevented him doing so.

If the secret is embedded in another person's own ability, how can it ever be yours?

Many believe that O-Sensei was the benevolent guardian of the great secrets by which means he achieved what he did. In fact, he tried his best to share them but often left his students puzzled. Many follow in his footsteps hoping that they too will find this illusive 'magic'. Is it a path to within self or to somewhere far beyond? How much of it is physicality, how much, the application of mind. How much is of the spirit?

How readily we use the words *harmony of spirit* to describe our art but do we really understand what spirit is? Without knowing what it is, how can we then find harmony? Are we tripped up by the invisible? Is finding spirit one of the true secrets?

We might well think, 'I know what spirit is,'
and so we might - until we are asked to explain.

The feelings you experience on gaining lesser secrets can still be quite euphoric, as if you were the only one. Even if millions had known this before you, it still feels like your discovery because, in part, it is just that. How many times has someone confided in you their great secret and you thought, 'I knew that already but hadn't made the connection.'

"There are secrets, then there are secrets that you are told, but they remain secrets because you don't understand them." *Tim Buswell in 2009*

The implication of a secret is that it is something being withheld from you by another, yet all unknowns are secrets and some unknowns will stay that way for eternity.

Peter R, also 2009, had sought the secrets for and by his self, he was invincible, finding his freedom had led him to places where energy became visible to him, even the strongest man present could not hold him; he was at peace with who he was and where he was. His freedom to experiment, study and practise without constraint led him to understand what others see as secrets. So, although we need a teacher, it can be the shadow of that same teacher that shackles you to certitude and prevents your own discoveries. You can never know his secret; you can only find your own.

Consider then, there is a secret, a true secret that is beyond ordinary human understanding. We even know what it is - it is something which cannot be taught, nor explained in words. As O-Sensei said,

"The Gods will not allow it."

"Inward truths and mysteries are inevitably secret for those, who lack the faculty to perceive them."

W. *Wilmshurst.*

X.

Become calm, become quieter, and all that was always known to you will be revealed, and when it is, you will never explain it, for such words do not exist in the thinking world. Hence the old saying,

"He who speaks does not know,
he who knows does not speak."

A true secret is exactly that ... something subtle, powerful and indescribable.

"We sit around in a ring and suppose. But the secret sits in the middle and knows."

Robert Frost

You'll seek peace in the world and discover only illusion,
for peace can only reside in those who walk that path.

***

23. Aikido ... martial art ?

'We can only ever hear
what our understanding allows us to hear.'

So how deep goes our understanding? Is aikido a martial art? In fact, what is a martial art? Is aikido an effective self defence against street crime? Are we truly honest when we examine our abilities and when we teach students? Do we examine deeply enough our understanding of the art we follow, or even at all? Do we visit other clubs and styles, moving out of our comfort zone, or do we think we have all the answers we need?

There are those who, though advancing well in aikido, decide that there is more to learn from somewhere or something else and they explore Cheng hsin, Systema, tai chi, or other arts, even yoga. What is it that makes them look elsewhere? From my observations, they usually find what they were seeking and what was evidently missing from their aikido journey. Often those other groups help and support each other better than we do in the so called aikido 'community'.

There are also those in the world that criticise us for calling our art 'self defence' and they say what we do is more akin in nature to the tea ceremony. Do they have a point?

Shouldn't we be more resistant to the trend of insularity and being competitive between styles, organisations and clubs? Why allow the 'others' to become the enemy in an art that seeks harmony? Is this really what O-Sensei sought? Yet we say we follow him and do this in his name?

Profound but so true is an old Chinese saying,

'Seeing is never seeing'.

Couldn't we work together more and help each other promote the art of aikido.
Aikido offers us:- An exercise system, training in aspects of self defence, developing health defence, improving confidence, body awareness, mind body co-ordination, social and self awareness, balance and power, spiritual advancement and even engagement in a pathway to moving meditation and above all a sense of peace.

"Aikido is not a technique to fight with or defeat the enemy. It is the way to reconcile the world and make human beings one family." Morihei Ueshiba, Founder of Aikido.

Also...

". . . comparisons of O-Sensei's sword work with classical sword schools are completely beside the point as his intention was not to impart battlefield techniques but to show how divine energy channels through the human body, the space around it, and all throughout the Universe."
From the Aikido Journal Newsletter, March 17, 2015

Such arts are mechanisms to improve life, yours!

Learning from the experience of your own practise, question in your own mind if what you read and see makes sense to you; for

you are the map maker of your own world,
you are, your own destiny.

***

24. Aikido and cross training.

Stick your ego in the cupboard and go and visit another club, another teacher, even another art and find out if they have something to which you were previously blind. How arrogant are we if we look down on others of lower rank and think, "they have nothing to teach me." Go and find out, and be prepared for an awful shock.

I cannot help feeling that O-Sensei, who none of us are ever likely to emulate, found his answers from diverse sources, dare I say, even from his farming practises, never mind martial training. Yet many of us think to find our own answers by aikido alone. True, we follow our own way in life but is your aikido the real thing? Can you make it work? Indeed, is that last question indicative of a non aiki attitude in itself? Think about that a moment or two.

We may be strong, capable and very good at what we do and though it may not be correct, time and practise has made us effective despite any defect. It's even worse if we never train with other styles or clubs (or even other arts). Safe and stuck in our comfort zone we deny ourselves the opportunity to grow. Yes, at times this can be depressing or uncomfortable. O-Sensei never stopped studying and exploring the mind body connection, yet how body aware are we?

Will aikido give us conscious body awareness? If we don't let rank get in the way, a visit to another teacher may well bring a discovery to our advantage. But that challenges our sense of accomplishment, it rattles at the cage of our comfort zone.

After some 40 years of training, I am now more amazed at what I **cannot** do than what I **can** do.

A few years back, I joined a large number of teachers from across the world at an all embracing seminar of aikido in Burwell, Cambs. An event promoted by Quentin Cooke for Aiki Extensions. I witnessed how a beginner, with only one lesson behind them, using true principles was more effective than I was with all my years of techniques.

I had become a prisoner of what I knew. Freedom sometimes presents a more challenging environment.
I'm not going to rabbit on about this but as older age approaches I have less fear about being open with my words.
Many of us have forgotten what aikido really is and some of us never even knew in the first place.
At the very least, think on that also for a moment or two.

The Chinese have a worthy saying,

"Don't just accept – go see."

***

25. Martial arts compared with dangerous occupations – comparing the principles.

Maintain a safe and guarded posture, regardless of it being visible to others.
Develop all around awareness and sensitivity to any advancing danger.
Your intuition improves and a sixth sense develops about potential dangers.
Remain calm and focussed throughout.
Be adaptable and react intelligently to change.
Train well and often.
Promote the will to serve others.
Stand resolutely between others and danger.
Develop trust and respect, for they are reciprocal.
Convey only meaningful information.
Practise realistically and for any situation.
Train your spirit as well as your body.
Develop self discipline.

The quality of your actions and deeds become more important than the façade of ego.
At the core you find an empathy with others, a shared sense of brother/sisterhood regardless of creed, colour or nationality.
Aspire to being better, in your actions as well as within self. A good reputation must be earned.
Cultivate a deeper and ultimately beneficial appreciation of responsibility for your own actions.
Consequences become a reality in your life.

With luck, you live through it all and the very act of living through it, becomes reward in itself.
Techniques and consequences may vary but the principles, the real essence of each activity are likely the same. Facing up to risks to your health in any form raises your awareness to the value of life itself.
Wouldn't you agree?

***

26. Choosing a way to train with weapons in line with the principles.

Based on my many years of training in the Aiki weapons of Saito Sensei from my own teacher Sensei Tony Sargeant, years of tai chi practise and some very useful insights into Ki Aikido from Sensei Huw Collingbourne, I'd like to share some thoughts on training with weapons.
The Iwama style weapons training has given a foundation of techniques and applications. Their purpose is to change the body, express and extend spirit and develop skills in timing and distance. Tai chi has brought a philosophy and a set of principles that sit in harmony with my idea of aikido.

The symbol we so often associate with tai chi represents opposites that abide in harmony not in conflict. The symbol has no beginning and no end; there are no straight lines and no breaks.

The principles of Ki aikido, difficult to master as they are, offer abilities that seem at times, akin to magic.
(Essential though that you find the right teacher, the right magician.)

Would you agree that aikido requires sensitivity, connectivity and relaxation of the right kind, to effect the desired result on your training partner? Are Aiki principles generally counter intuitive to the human condition? This is also its greatest asset. Training with weapons is an interesting and useful way to develop the harmony necessary for aikido and can help find the effortless power exhibited by some of the great past masters.
Only the receiver experiences the force but is unable to identify clearly where it came from, rendering them unable to counter.
How often have you heard expressions like, 'accept the gift,' 'please come past,' 'care for the attacker,' 'respect the partner's ki,'? All these expressions are there to take your mind away from the point of contact and allow your whole being to engage in the movement without tension and in a harmonious manner that leads to an inability to harm or control you.

Success for you, is not over them,
but over yourself.

If aikido requires sensitivity and leading the attacker to where they are willing to go – not where you force them against their will – then to exert unnecessary force will be counter to aikido principles. Any force the attacker feels, not in line with their own, will provide them with information to use against you.

Like it or not, weapons training was a big part of O-Sensei's practise and the development of his art and his own amazing skills.
If harmony is required in taijutsu then it must be also found in weapons or bukiwaza.
Taking the Jo or short staff as our example, it should be possible to make all the suburi and kata with the lightest of grip and to experience the moment without any effort except intention. Whether you wish to hold stronger is up to you and circumstances. But, if you can perform katate tomauchi (suburi number 12) with only a light thumb and finger grip, then you must have been in harmony with the Jo. Both you and the Jo travelled on a mutually agreeable path. The sort of harmony that you need in taijutsu and for what I now believe is the essence of aikido. The passive overcomes the strong because it needs to find the right path. Yin overcomes yang.
All of your moves with weapons should take the path that is agreeable to the weapon. There are certain directions, almost exclusively along the length of the weapon, that provide that effortless path to aiki. The path when found is perfection.
The weapon is not used to block but to blend, connect and neutralise and your own movement should be at one with that blend.

***'Never have conflict at the point of contact'**,*
- our prevailing principle .

If you can't do it with the Jo, then perhaps you'll struggle to achieve it empty handed.
A harsh grip on the Jo can only slow and restrict your movements and possibly worse still, encourage you to make the Jo travel where you wish – whether right or wrong. Lighter grip means more sensitivity, more harmony, better feeling.
It's the body and not the arms, that makes the move whole, and in doing so, will affect the training partner in the same way too i.e. through their whole body.

Adjust your body to improve connection with the jo rather than stress the hands to do so.

I neither know nor claim that this view is right but it represents my current belief based on the feelings I have during training.

Perhaps you might find it worth a try.

27. A Warrior's Journey?

I have to say that it's somewhat of an embarrassing title to me, and that in itself unveils one of my own long struggles in life. However, I tell myself that this story is born not of reality but of dreams and that in itself makes it easier to write. The enemy within is real enough, the internal enemies of ego and greed, of doubt, embarrassment, fear of rejection and humiliation. These are enemies that transcend race, creed, age, gender or ability, we are all equally at their mercy; a mercy seldom if ever given and never offered. It's been a long journey during which time of travelling I have often been tested and so often defeated, sometimes without realisation, so subtle is the enemy.

The one I've attempted to follow for over 45 years now, had some ideas on this . . .

The penetrating brilliance of a sword
wielded by a follower of the Way
strikes at the evil enemy
lurking deep within - one's own body and soul.

Morihei Ueshiba

I woke early that Spring morning and gathered my belongings for the journey to yet another battlefield, for we always think it is some place else; yet unknowing, we carry it with us every

where we go. Spare clothes, uniform and weapons were duly packed in my vehicle and the day felt good.
The day was good and I felt good, even if a little aged and with the odd pain in my hands – I considered at some depth what it might be and how long it might last. However, in general, it was a good day on which to set off to fight my 'war', a war I live in hopes of winning one day. By win, I mean, to find peace within. There is no anger or sense of revenge, no hatred or angst – for they too are our enemy within. It will often be they that choose the field upon which you will metaphorically do or die.

"I count him braver who overcomes his desires, than him who conquers his enemies for the hardest victory is self."
Aristotle

Unusually the Sun is shining, if you live on the UK west coast you will know what I mean! The first part of the journey is without incident – all is peaceful – the world at large may be gripped in conflict but inside my car it was at peace. It's the only peace we can ever experience – our own.
The transport cafe was full of good natured drivers having their rest breaks. I ordered the large breakfast minus the beans and toast. Despite then being an advocate of the Palaeolithic diet, I accepted the fried potatoes.
There was no conflict between me and the potatoes. Though they were not on my 'list', in my heart they were not the enemy – not today. The motorways too were more peaceful this day; we all drove in harmony, all going the same way. (It helps, doesn't it?) The odd poor soul did cut across my path to take an exit for which they had prepared badly . . . or perhaps cleverly! I have to confess a curse did pass my lips, a pointless gesture as you will know yourself and it served only to damage me not them. My stress level was elevated, my immune system lowered and a few minutes of my life that could have been contented were otherwise made distraught.

The enemy within is a skilled and often smiling assassin, striking when the innocent is least ready.
The radio was tuned in to a pleasing programme, a gentle speaking man talked of quiet heroism in war; his chosen music was Amazing Grace with the band of the Scots Guards and Waltzing Matilda sung by a powerful and emotive Australian woman. Both were poignant and stirring music, as traditionally befits 'warriors' setting out to do battle.
I was travelling to meet with like minded colleagues, fellow warriors of the way.
They would be gathering in a harmony and friendship that can only be born of facing a common struggle. Each must fight their own battle but each would be bounded by others seeking the same success – comrades all.
United in a moment of peace, the uniformed warriors of the way with bright white gi and pressed black hakama, weapons ready but dormant by their sides, bow reverently to the founder's image and prevailing spirit. This is a brief encounter with real peace, humility and intention, this moment when they all bow together. Our leader stands before us, exalting us to do our best and to do only good in our efforts to defeat the enemy (within).
This was not a beginning, nor was it an end for it would often appear that our journey has neither.
The experienced warrior shares hard won knowledge to keep others safe, because at some time and for some reason they felt those others needed to know. But perhaps do not **need** to know; perhaps they do not **want** to know.
And so our warrior finds yet another battle, the one that requires coming to terms with it being their journey and theirs alone.
In any event, regardless of our ambitions, our glorious victories or shameful defeats we must make the most of our days on the path.

"The waving of the summer grass is all that remains of the dreams and ambitions of long dead warriors."

Japanese poet, Basho

***

28. Are you prepared?

When facing your partner in ***preparation*** for practise you should already have been in a state of ***awareness*** long before.

If you have to prepare
then you were never ready

However, in being ready, do not tense or give away your readiness to the attacker.
Your kens should not touch prior to the practise itself, for had they touched, one of you should have taken the energy and entered.
The fact that kens touch and no action ensues is an indicator that neither partners were truly ready. How often might you have heard the click clack of ken against ken ... sometimes even followed by a knowing embarrassment and apology ... then the teacher calls out again, 'First kumitachi, three times and change.'

***

'The faintest pencil is more powerful than the greatest mind.'

***

29. Can this be the 'magic' in Aikido?

It's a little known but natural phenomenon called the *'ideomotor effect'* and has been written about before with regard to aikido, particularly in relationship to ki power. Simply put, muscles in the body join in with a person's will or belief without informing that same person they have done so. The person will be unaware that the muscles engaged, in fact they might even argue that they were relaxed at the time – they will not be aware of the underlying muscle involvement.

I've added a beautiful drawing of a tai chi posture (single whip) but it is only the knees I ask you to consider. I think we can agree that the knees are bent and therefore 'closing'.

If this were so then the strain would be enormous, but the practitioner would probably say that they felt no such strain and might even go on to say that they were comfortable and relaxed in this posture. Take a break from reading and try it for yourself if you wish. (No liability taken by the author!)

This is what I think she is doing; this is my understanding . . . as the knees bend and begin closure, her mind is doing the opposite, it is telling the knees to open. This in turn will trigger the *ideomotor effect* and bring muscles into play which balance the posture – balanced = no strain. We tend to think the mind is doing it, but the mind is triggering muscles to act on our behalf without us knowingly engaging them.
This is one of the reasons we should at least look at other styles of aikido. Take Ki aikido or at least Koichi Tohei's view on it. There may be many teachers out there who do not commonly practise 'ki exercises', perhaps don't even know about them!

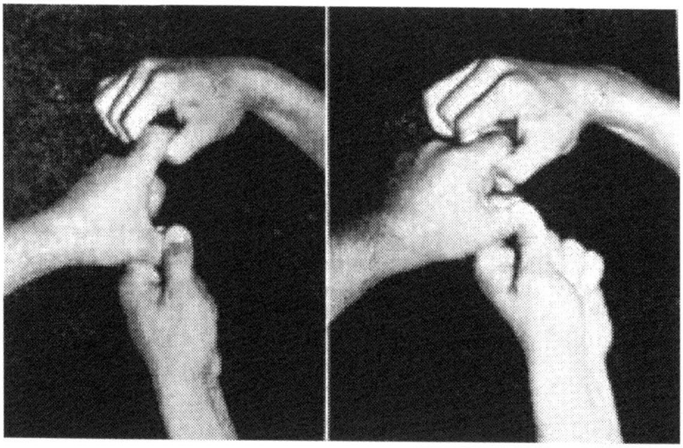

Here I've taken a picture from *Aikido in Daily Life,* showing thumb and finger held together, once by physical and known strength and the other relaxed but using mind power. The object of the exercise is to see which remains intact after a partner tries to pull them apart. By imagining that the fingers make an iron ring they prove the most powerful. Power without effort.

How do you think the 'unbendable arm' exercise works? We never really question it, because it is the magic ingredient 'ki' isn't it? Well perhaps it is in a way. The better your mind is trained in channelling belief the better,

the more relaxed your muscles,

the easier your energy can flow.

Success in the practice breeds more belief and therefore greater success . . . but we continue to feel no physical feed back – in fact we feel even less. The big guy falls over and you wonder why he did, as you hadn't put any physical effort into the technique yet.

What about the age old story of the woman who lifts a car to save a child, yet afterwards cannot explain how. In such a case, instinctive and long hidden nature kicks in, maternal instinct, adrenalin and unity of mind, body and spirit combine with an unbreakable intent to achieve – simple as that. That's why we can't do it in ordinary life – because of how we are educated to grow up (eg, 'sit up straight!), nothing is connected up properly and our mind interferes with our true ability and causes doubt to act against our hidden powers. Don't do it, but you could go outside and try and lift your car now . . . doubt has already defeated you as you walk to the door. The martial arts are a pathway to change some of that. (Don't expect to replace the car jack any time soon !)

The ***ideomotor effect*** also throws light on how another person can detect your intentions. Hiding what you intend to do requires some skill and practise. Remember, almost imperceptible muscle movements will occur the moment you create mind intent. Ever wondered why some people have 'seen' your attack coming so early that your attack has to follow and try and catch up – leading to your downfall? (Boxers can avoid punches that are so fast they shouldn't be able to – they have read the signals that precede the physical action). Highly skilled martial artists see these minuscule indications of intent, perhaps not consciously but at a deeper level they themselves cannot explain.

Ki exercises are one way to enhance your natural abilities. Call it what you like, even magic if you will, but it does exist and can be trained.

In conclusion;

Ki extension and relaxation = power.

Ki – imagination – belief gives birth to power – the energy can increasingly become a tangible reality.

Like in the tai chi practitioner's knees or the finger joints in Tohei's exercise, the joints are open, relaxed – it is the space between that allows the 'magic' to travel.

"In nothingness, there is everything."

You only need to ask your mind to take you there !

It's only my opinion . . . but I'm happy with it . . . so far !

***

O-Sensei said: "In aikido, there is absolutely no attack. To attack means that the spirit has already lost. We adhere to the principle of absolute non-resistance, that is to say, we do not oppose the attacker. Thus, there is no opponent in aikido. The victory in aikido is *masakatsu agatsu* (correct victory, self-victory); since you win over everything in accordance with the mission of heaven, you possess absolute strength."

***

'Neurophysiologist Benjamin Libet [in 1983] conducted experiments to explore free will, the inner experience of sensation, thought and emotion. If you have free will, what you want to think or act, you think or act freely: all from your consciousness, [you are] will free. This is why a teacher becomes a stumbling student in a new teacher's class. No free will.' By *Jow Yuzo*

30. More on relaxation - because It's probably not quite what you think it is.

Relaxation allows extension of the body and opening the joints. Relaxation enables energy to flow and there is more 'mind' to it than we often think or use. It is less 'willpower' but more a subtle imagination or belief that is required. Willpower can create its own tensions and blocks.

A relaxed body is a united body and therefore has more power.

It is well said,

"where intention goes, energy flows",

but examine carefully the possible differences between where your energy goes and where your intention goes. Intention may be one directional (put simply) but energy may be expanding in all directions. The Chinese express it as Ba Men or eight gates, each of them opening in a different direction. Open them all.

Your imagination or belief for want of better description can also lead your energy or ki in other directions too, like spirals and circles and even at some distance from your body.

***

"In true Budo there are no opponents –
seek to be one with all things."

***

31. Once upon a time in Kefalonia.

I watched Sensei Sargeant demonstrate different levels of understanding and speak of his discoveries. As I watched and listened, the sense and truth of it was apparent, but I am unable to express it in words – it is simply a personal journey of discovery to be found in our own time and place ... and only if we want to. A bit like a holiday snap of a beach or a tree, they mean little to anyone else ... other than those who have been there. At a certain level the practice of jo kata can almost seem like a more expressive version of counting prayer beads.

So, as my porridge cools and the island of Kefalonia warms in the Sun, I conclude that the Jo in all its forms is merely a companion to you on your path, the path, which like the kata, remains the same – a spiritual path – a journey of the higher self with the rest of you joining in as required .... if not, then perhaps the path and Jo are not for you.

***

Section 2. Technical and practical section.

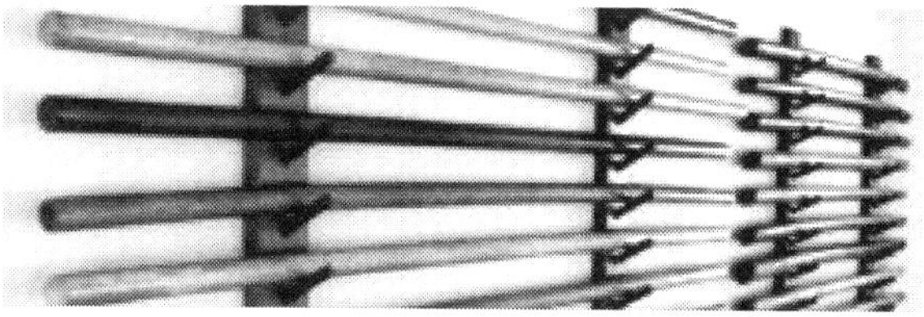

Boken for precision, Jo for flowing, the essence of each, inherent in the body and spirit of one who walks the path of aikido - way of harmony of spirit.

***

32. Jo description and advice

The Jo is a short staff, good ones are made of Japanese Oak, its length varies with the user (from the ground to just under the armpit). Because of its length and the opportunity to use both ends, it can be used in carrying out techniques from Bo (long staff), sword and spear. It is evident in each case which

weapon is being represented by the jo. Eg Ki style 22 jo kata, if you look carefully it fits easily into spear practice.
Using the Jo involves relaxed postures and movements except for the moment of impact and perhaps then too.
Being relaxed allows quicker movement, more whole body co-ordination and a degree of flexibility should the need arise to change direction.
The founder had three parts to his art called aikido:
1. Body techniques
2. The Ken, a wooden sword
3. The Jo, a wooden staff

They were used to achieve simple understanding. Saito Sensei (9th Dan) said 'when you use the weapons think of body movements; when you use body movements think of the weapons.'

***

33. When practising ken variations, (*henka*),
here shown is a henka from the first kumitachi.

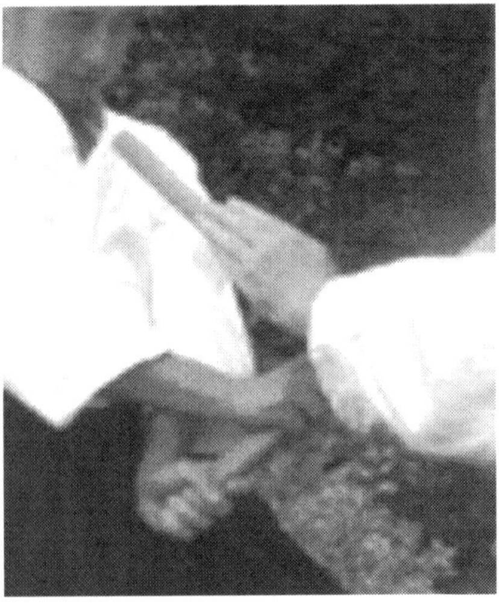

Make sure you keep your ***thumb and fingers*** in a safe place ....if you want to keep them anyway.

34. The basics of the Aiki Ken

The basics of the Aiki Ken are centered on the suburi and kumitachi. Familiarity with these fundamentals leads to an ability to acquire more advanced skills such as tachi dori or "sword taking" techniques

Look straight ahead.

Don't open the front foot too far, or on occasion not at all, when changing posture as it will detrimentally effect hip movement on strike. (Some might say only use hips, certainly greater speed is available when initiating from hips.)

Narrow posture, as if walking a bridge parapet.

Pelvic tilt needs to be understood fully to make it effective and safe. (It is easily possible to exagerate the movement and cause yourself harm in the left hip joint. Always avoid extremes.)

Leading foot lands toes first, heel lands with end of boken cut.

Suburi is mind of no mind, do not think 'cut' but seek perfection of movement, complete peace and harmony with body and spirit. Just do - don't think.

Elbows not wider than shoulders.

Your cut will be more powerful if you are relaxed.

Left hand provides power, right hand provides guidance.

It is the hip movement that provides the power that is transmitted through the hands.

35. Morihiro Saito Sensei:

Aikido is generally believed to represent circular movements. Contrary to such belief however, aikido in its true Ki form, is a fierce art piercing straight through the centre of the opposition.

36. Furuya Sensei on Swordsmanship:

Letting go of the idea of "sword" and the idea of "action" is the meaning behind "willow in the gentle breeze." When the slight summer breeze blows, does the willow follow the "nature of the willow," or does it follow the "nature of the breeze?" Please think about this - in this lies the essence of sword technique.

***

37. Using Jo or Ken.

Explore the value of weapons practice in improving posture, balance, timing and distance in aikido practice.
Explore one or two examples of internal power that lead to a centred sense of peace in the practitioner.
Explore the value of non conflict with the point of contact – e.g. deflect a powerful Jo thrust with the lightest of grip.
The value of 'opposites'.
Seek principle based teaching and not just choreography.

Principles should be a constant even if politics, egos, opinions and learning are not.

We train slowly and purposefully in order that our bodies can inform our minds about what feels correct or not ...... and then change what is asked.

***

"Your most dangerous opponents are fear, anger, confusion, doubt and despair."

***

38. Observation of posture.

My friend, Mark Allcock Sensei,
founder of Wellsprings Aikido Club.

Observe:-
Hips engaged. Eyes engaged. Body centred.
Joints aligned. Expanding energy. Circles and spirals. Connectedness. Martial. Awareness. Preparedness. Spirit. Movement in stillness.

A worthy posture and attitude to copy.

***

39. Wise words from Karate 6th Dan Bill Hollister.

The principles may be unchanging but everything else is. Keep an open mind and test ideas for yourself.
Training with weapons ensures co-ordination of both hands - through the connection of weapon, they learn to be in harmony.
Weapons training ensures that both sides of the body are trained.
Weight and length of the wooden long weapons ensures the receptive body can train and adapt to avoid inefficient posture.

***

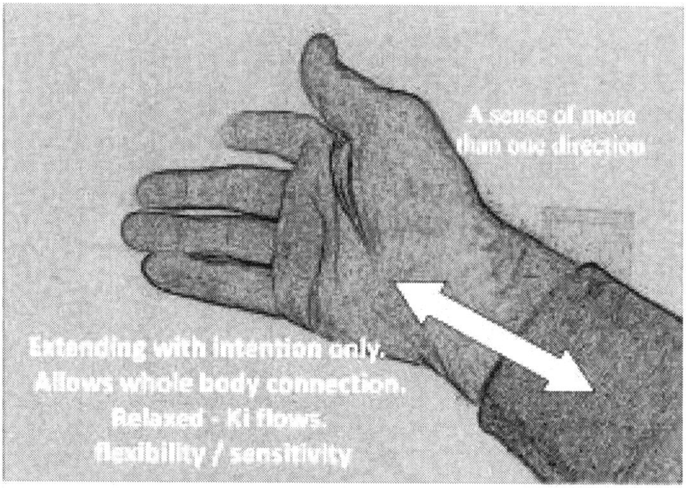

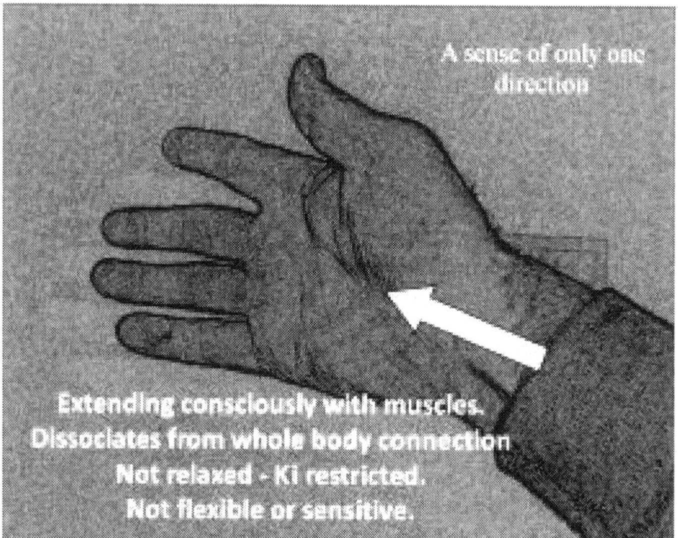

40. Extending with intention.

41. Jo and its origins.

Miyamoto Musashi was Japan's greatest ever swordsman and put many duellists in an early grave.
Legend tells us that Muso Gonnosuke Katsuyoshi defeated him with a wooden stick (Jo). In so doing, he gave birth to a martial arts system that would elevate the humble wooden staff to one of the pre eminent weapons of the bugei (combat techniques) of Japan.

***

42. Safety first.

Jo – almost any stick will do for practising your own moves and choreography, however, for partner work, particularly Jo dori and Jo nage, an oak Jo is less likely to break. A broken Jo can become a razor sharp dagger. Small splinters can spread on the mat. Even an oak Jo should be checked carefully for damage before each use. Not by carelessly running your hand down it!

***

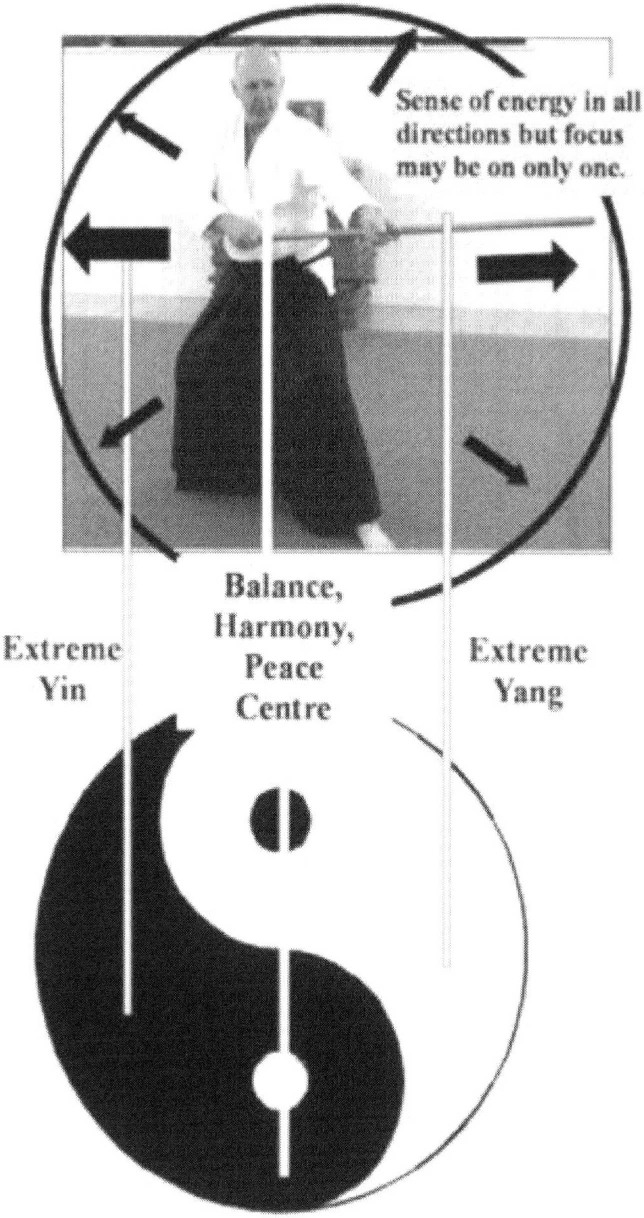

43. A picture of harmony.

44. A few practical Jo reminders.

Lone practice can lead to an ***imagined*** world of greatness.
Partner practice can lead to a ***new reality*** – a reality where ability, posture, spirit and timing are all put to question.
Progressively your greater skills lead to having fun, fun for the ego as Jo whacks Jo and you win. Conversely sadness when you lose .... But there'll always be a next time - or so you think.
Then a reminder comes your way that ***Aiki means harmony of spirit***, and that your path is to beat the enemy within, not the one without.
Try not to strain the body when practising, as best you can ***remain relaxed and in good posture***.
Good posture requires ***good foundations***.
Hold the Jo firmly but not so tightly that it creates tensions, neither so loosely that it can be knocked from your hands.
Little finger should be able to grip comfortably.
Remember that it is not the Jo that does the work but you. The Jo is merely an ***extension of the body***.
Blend, deflect or neutralise your partner while ***retaining your own power***, which remains hidden from them until the moment of application.
At the ***point of application*** never feel your own power coming back to you. Only your 'opponent' or partner should experience your power.
Do not think of ***winning ... or losing***.... Merely make the correct movements that lead to the proper conclusion. It is on your journey and not the destination you should keep an eye .
Keep your thumbs and fingers safe !

Fighting distance and blending skills will all benefit from Jo practice. The power and possibilities of an opponent wielding a Jo serve to sharpen the mind.

Minimise movement – don't add your own flowery bits..... keep it simple.
In general the ***hips*** should move before the Jo.
All movement starts from ***centre.***
Don't over commit --- every move you make should be ***recoverable***. This can relate to your own position or one you have in relation to your partner.
Safe practice means avoiding attacks to throat, knee, groin, jaw bone etc, however, ***martially*** these are the very targets you would seek .... But this conflicts with Aiki.

Place your spirit **through** the Jo, this connects you to its very end and beyond and not just where you are gripping.
Give 80% effort, ***saving something for yourself***, give less than 50% effort and you waste your time.
Hard ***training*** is not necessarily training hard ... put your whole self into the study, mind body and spirit ... look to see how you could improve, feel how you could improve ... and do it.
Using weapons correctly can develop good, habit formed, integrity of posture that is transferable to empty hand techniques. It is a key purpose behind weapons practice . . . to cultivate and develop the body and not merely to become a sword or stick fighter.

Similar advice is given below, a worth while repetition.

Good advice deserves repetition.

***

45. Positioning and strength of grip on Jo.

Always add a spiral for added power, even if unnoticed by observers. Use body not arms. Remain centred, extending Ki in different directions (your body will willingly join in with your mind's intent)

Remain relaxed but connected throughout your body as well as in movement. Internal power can be enhanced by cross body connection. Extend spirit beyond end of Jo. Avoid feeling your own power regardless of how great it might feel - when you can feel it, it can be used against you. You don't even have to grip the Jo to move your opponent. When feet, hips, shoulders and hands are in harmony with the alignment of the Jo and you remain centred, you maximise your soft power. (approximating horse stance assists in whole body connection). Use of hips may be easier understood by thinking 'hip crease'.

Remember that the hand grip on the jo should be soft enough that someone can turn it in your hands but tight enough that they cannot take it from you.

If at any time you feel the need to prepare -
then you were never ready !

If you are not sensitive enough to harmonise with the weapons, and become 'one' with them . . . that is, a partnership not a dictatorship, then how can weapons be correctly training the body for Aikido ?

It is an abiding principle - the weapons are there to change your body.

How, is the question.

***

46. How and why to train with Jo and Ken in Aikido.

It's much easier to understand thoughts than it is to write them down, but I'll have a try. We can only believe what our mind accepts and only feel what our body allows. Please explore this section and see how much you might or might not find agreeable. Everything in here can be tested by yourself, therefore you can make up your own mind of its worth.
O-Sensei must have trained with and used weapons like Jo and Ken, (also spear and bayonet) for a reason. He developed techniques to counter weapons too and more than a few of the taijutsu techniques have their origins in this field. If you do not have a partner skilled in the use of weapons then how can you hope to develop such skills as O-Sensei yourself?

As a student of aikido, isn't O-Sensei's word good enough for you or are you only looking for part of his art? (Perhaps I am guilty of this too in my pursuit of weapons training.) How can our martial art be complete without at least some weapons training?

Practising with weapons can also simply be great fun, and why should it not be so? Why not smile and be happy?

Weapons practice is something you can do almost anywhere, either alone or with a partner. (walking stick, umbrella, broom handle etc) Hiring halls and having expensive mats is not a requirement.

You have as much freedom with weapons as the art of aikido may have whispered to your soul when you first took up the art. (Garden, beach, forest – but beware Public places in case the armed response unit is called by overzealous busy-bodies . . . a true story)

I hesitate to put in a 'do not', for it is rarely if ever helpful, but, if you only use your arms to move the weapons then you are merely enjoying or enduring some exercise, you will not be doing aikido. Your whole body needs to be connected and involved and better still, your mind as well. Do not isolate your arms from the rest of you. (yet I know someone who can and be highly successful doing it - so there is much to still learn.)

Act from the centre, not the extremities.

Although we are told to move from the centre it is a more usefully applied mechanism to engage with the hip joint by mindfully emphasising the 'kua' or hip crease. At a higher level the hip might move less, yet energy still flows through.

Training with weapons teaches your body a wide ranging variety of co-ordinated and flowing movements that can prepare you for the dynamic changes of postures required during tai jutsu.

Sensei Sergei Stoliarov

Using weapons correctly can develop good, habit formed, integrity of posture that is transferable to empty hand techniques. It is a key purpose behind weapons practice . . . to cultivate and develop the body and not merely to become a sword or stick fighter.

Weapons help to teach 'open' postures and offer a narrow, smaller target to the attacker but allow longer reach and generate greater power for the defender. Training with weapons is a useful mechanism to develop correct connection through your body and also to extend your mind. Ask yourself, "When I lift Ken or Jo above my head, can I relax my shoulders any more than they are . . . even just a little?"

If the answer is 'yes' then, when you lifted the weapon, you disconnected your arms from your body in the 'energetic' connective sense. You also moved the shoulder joint from a place of its own relaxed centre to a place of extremes.

Weapons or not, properly relaxed and centred joints are an asset, if not essential, for good aikido. Weapons can help you find this place; a place that encourages internal power to exist and energetic power to flow.

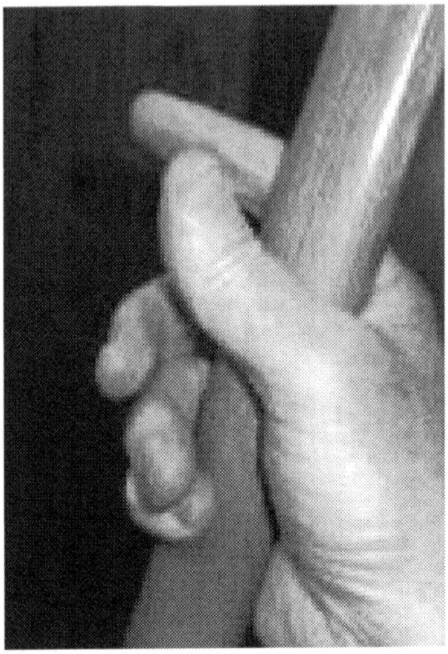

Using weapons can develop an efficient and natural gripping that maximises your potential at a level you may not have yet considered. The 5 'fingers' are controlled by two separate nerve systems. The little finger and ring finger are connected by the ulna nerve; other fingers are not connected to the ulna nerve but to a separate system. The little finger system is more active than the first finger system; activation of the little finger tends towards mind body relaxation, the feet flatten and the inner thigh muscles release. Whereas, use of the thumb, first and middle fingers causes the body to become substantial, the feet to press into the ground and inner thigh muscles to contract the body in action. Gripping with little finger first also embodies a sense of gripping from your own centre.

Perhaps your grip should be invisible to yourself?
When you feel your own power, it is coming back to you and can therefore be used against you.

When using aiki weapons, when we lift we need a relaxed grip and relaxed body and the grip tends to be from little fingers first, roundly encompassing the Jo or Ken ...... even during the strike the hands are comfortable and relaxed as is the body, ... Then as the 'strike' materializes it is a time for change, a fuller grip engaging thumb and first two fingers develops. Power is issued from a fully active and more substantial body. However, you should always seek calm and relaxation because real power resides there.

Consider this. At the end of a ken strike we are advised to rotate both grips inwards to the centre, as if wringing out a wet towel. Now, we could do that simply physically but how much better if it is the mind that 'sees' the wringing out and the ideomotor effect itself operates the muscles. This way the action is completed without any felt tension. Tension is a result of antagonistic muscles engaged therefore not in harmony.

Using ken and Jo develops the circles and spirals which can then more clearly be observed due to exaggeration of movement in weapons. Thus enhancing the benefits and correcting faults.

Weapons training increases awareness and martial attitude as well as developing a greater understanding in fighting distance or **ma-ai.**

Weapons also greatly increase awareness of consequences: - is the Jo or ken safely parried or is the thumb or wrist broken? This is a fine line indeed.

Facing fears helps to develop better self control and the student's reaction speeds are necessarily improved.

Lifting the ken or Jo can also be good for your general health, especially if carried out correctly, consciously and combined with breath. Any exercise that involves raising arms and breathing in, is good for the internal organs. (Compare with some Chi Kung exercises.) The arms should remain powerful, not by muscular tension but by a power motivated by the mind; they become the 'iron bar in cotton wool'. Arms are neither collapsed nor rigid but have found a middle way that is more born of mind than physicality. It is the relaxed concentration you may have heard about before. There is extension in the feeling at all times, even when the arms are bent they do not 'come back' to you. If your arm is soft (collapsing) it will be pushed back to you and if your arm is rigid it will be used to push you back.

If you extend your arm with intention it is still possible to bend it, as long as you maintain extension and an opening in the joints (thus only appearing to observers that it comes back to you). There is a world of difference. The overall length of the arm should stay the same regardless of any change in elbow angle.

Weapons training will teach you relaxation in movement while under pressure. For example:- in the 3rd kumitachi the more relaxed the defensive parry is made, the more powerful a deflection it makes on the attacker's own strike. There is a case for, less muscle – more power. Cease to look outside for the effect of weapons but look in to yourself, and experience the effect. Seek to be one with the universe and do not fixate on an attacking weapon for it can do nothing without the person behind it.

Finally, perhaps this can also help.

Ai Ki Do. Ki is the so called magical ingredient and becomes seemingly more so to those who feel its effects without understanding them.

Ki is the essence of the art and the essence of a powerful, healthy body. You'll have to think of it what you will; there are lots of 'definitions' and opinions out there. Just keep it simple and know that there is some force at work which you might be able to harness to your advantage. Searching for it is part of your journey.

I'll call it 'spirit energy'; Ki is real and can, from the application of mind on a relaxed body, create a physical effect merely by its presence. Importantly, it does not work the other way – any tense physical activity actually stifles or shuts down the flow of Ki. There are lots of exercises that emphasise this point. I am sure you will know many yourselves; unbendable arm is a well known example. The objective of practising such exercises is surely to develop them in a manner that can be useful to you in your martial art or in daily life.

When you pick up the ken or Jo, add nothing more to that effort than that which is required to lift or move the weapon. By adding no extra, which becomes a stifling force, your energy can flow. Remember, it is the flow of this energy which animates real power (not strength, which is very different from power). Your energy can flow from your centre all the way to your hands and beyond.

Maintaining consciousness in hands is an asset.

By training in weapons you can access a useful tool to develop this mechanism. This is experientially true, regardless of what you really think about Ki.

My advice? Put the Ki in your aikido and put good weapons training back in while you are at it

O-Sensei surely didn't use weapons for nothing.

Sergei Stoliarov (left) Tony Sargeant sensei (right)

47. On training with weapons.

The following is my interpretation of advice given me in a conversation with my friend, Karate 6th Dan Sensei William Hollister (founder of Tamar Tai Chi).
From the viewpoint of an aikido student, it would be hard to differ in opinion. But, what do you think?

'Understand the weapon you are using or facing. Take into account if it is bladed or blunt. Consider this, even when using wooden 'bladed' weapons.
You cannot 'cut' with a blunt weapon; however, its action may follow a similar line at times in order to better protect your own wrists and joints. With weapons you learn about blocks . . . and whether they are useful or should instead be deflections.
Angles of attack and defence vary with the type of weapon.
Using weapons conditions the body, developing endurance, balance, power and co-ordination. It is a conditioning that only requires the presence of self and the weapon; this is one of its advantages.
Using weapons trains the mechanics of the body; weapons are a very useful aid to developing good footwork and maintaining centre.
Imagery, using your mind, of an opponent is required in the beginning to create correct focus, posture and movement. Flailing about with the weapon without such thought will be of little benefit.
Develop control; i.e. stop where and when you want to, and not when the weapon decides.
Hit what you aim for, even if imaginary. Know what to strike, when training alone use mirror imagery.
When training, be delicate and conscious; do not miss out any of the ingredients. There should be no weakness in your actions. . . none at all.
Consider the origins.

Original intent may have come from weapon to weapon.
If training a Kata, and there are many and various, know what it's all about; know why it is this or that move.
Have purpose in your Kata . . . always know 'why'.
Weapons training will reinforce the importance and necessity of mental focus.
Test your mind on adaptability and try movements or kata from both left and right sides or try part of a kata starting from the normal finish point. (Just as an exercise.)
A relaxed mind and body will come from much training.
Extension of body is good but tension in body is not.
Weapons training can enhance the awareness of breath in the whole issue. Breath is required as part of movement.
Kiai can become part of this; however, I suspect there is still much more for us to know on this topic, in that kiai should be there to take the opponent's mind and not your own. Neither should it create a tension in your own body but instead, in theirs.'

{Thank you Bill.}

***

"In the hands of a serious student, weapons are a pathway and a prayer towards balance and peace."

My good friend Terry, (Karate 4th Dan)

***

48. Tai chi and Aiki principles.

Mind moves body same as Tohei's exercises.
Push using inside muscles not outer and later push using energy.
Push resistance increases when using 'two bodies' by internalising a separation (there are 5 levels !)
Being heavy through being light – only feet feel weight.

Use of hip crease (kua) more to it than is obvious.
Avoiding double weighting (a state of the body when someone can easily push you.)
Joints open, muscles relaxed.
Using your body affects another's body. (using your back affects their back but if only using arms you will only affect their arms and therefore not be effective.)
Respecting the attacker
Avoiding direct action on the point of contact.
Power of connected relaxation ... Jo parry can be extremely effective if done with body and not just arms.

Ideas on ***unifying the body posture to generate more power*** .... ***more power means less effort*** ... believe it or not.
The ideas shown below are my own, so don't blame my teachers. However, it does fit with what we call an 'internal' art.
Firstly though, the knees . . . made to move more or less in one direction or plane. The knee joint will not be comfortable if bent in other directions or twisted .. ask your own knees, they will tell you.
So my advice is to align the knee centre with the middle of the foot . . . the long toes. Don't bend the knees beyond vertical lower leg.

Photo on the right, below:- I'm trying to show that you can set up a ***'circle of connection and therefore power between the opposite arm and hip, i***.e. right hip and left arm as shown in the picture. The same is done for the other opposites (right arm and left hip). It is hard to explain but I'll try ... the hip crease is drawn in a little but the feeling has to be that it is still opening .. almost as if it feels it is going forward, which results in the energy making an arc .... part going to the ground and part raising the ribs slightly. I think this is valid but represents my opinion only.

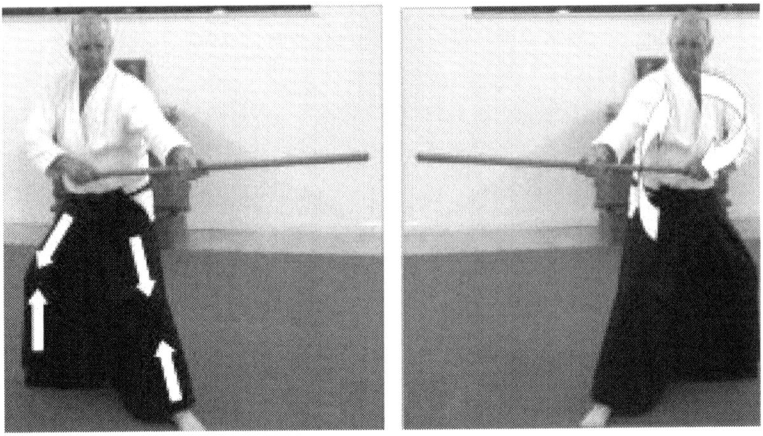

An attempt to show internal power connections in Tsuki

***

49. Ideomotor effects are involuntary motor movements that are performed by a person because of expectations, suggestions or preconceptions.
The person is not aware that they are causing the movements; therefore they ascribe the movement to an external force or power. The movement feels unnatural.
The "external forces" perceived are usually thought of as being paranormal in nature.
Much of aikido owes its success to this phenomena

***

50. Historical significance - the staff

The short wooden staff - throughout history one of man's greatest friends.
To test the depth of water, reach high berries and fruits, an aid to walking and climbing, a tool, a weapon, something to raise to the heavens and connect with the Gods. Shepherds carried

them, great warriors carried them, men of all persuasions.
Find that connection with nature and history .

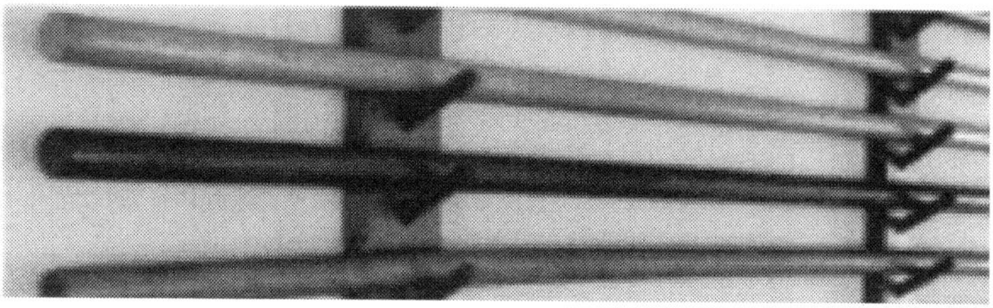

***

51. Uke's grip can teach bad habits.

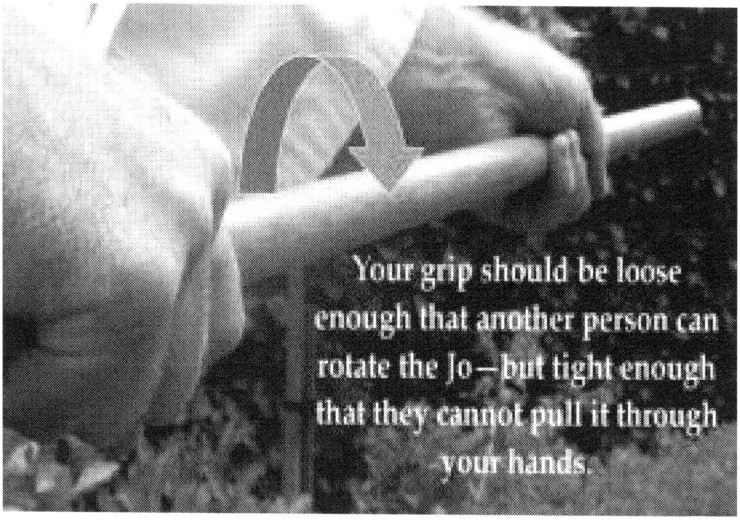

There shouldn't be any struggle in gripping and no joint should be pushed to the edge of movement. No self inflicted stress on body, just relaxed harmony throughout. No message sent either to self or opponent. If your hands cannot close comfortably around the jo then adjust your body shape to allow the grip to change rather than force your hands into position.

52. Something to consider on 'being centred'.

What is it that we understand about being centred? We surely have heard our teachers say, 'be grounded, be centred'. What is 'being centred'? Well, there are some obvious observations; the body should be upright and the centre of gravity should fall comfortably in the middle of the posture. The further you lean or shift your centre of gravity to one extreme or the other the less stable you are and the harder it is to execute fast moves like turning etc.

Perhaps there is more to it than the physical; take the eyes for example, not possible to move them into the back of your head physically ... but you can with the mind. Your eyes should be soft, soft focussed and appear to your mind that they are further back in your head ... near the ears .. and are looking out through the eye sockets from within and not from the front edge.

A mental sense of energy going in all directions also assists centring, front, back, left, right, up and down … your intention may be focussed in a particular direction ... as in Tsuki (thrust) but the sense that your energy expands from the centre in all directions should also exist. Exist in a state of no extremes.

Centred is also about being calm ... an essential feature of our art .... if not calm then you will be reaching out to one extreme or another ... it will fail to be balanced .. centred.

When moving your centre towards an opponent, they will sense the intent far more intuitively than visually. Move your centre - move their centre.

***

53. The student and the tatami (mat) – just one point of view among many.

'Hey, you haven't got any mats down.'

No, tonight we are practising weapons techniques, if it involves a throw we control to point of balance. It's quite simple. When their balance is taken they are no longer a threat.

'I can't train without mats.'

Why not? Why must you have mats?

'So we don't get hurt when we are thrown.'

Why do you have to be thrown? Aren't some of the techniques locks, even kotegaeshi can be used as a gently but persistently applied lock, it doesn't have to involve a throw and a high fall.

'You've only got to watch aikido on Youtube and you can see you need mats. . . otherwise the uke would be hurt due to the power of the throw.'

So, why does aikido require such hard throws? Isn't it good enough to harmonise, take uke's balance and gently place them in a position where they realise attack is futile?

'It's good fun to be thrown on the mat, gets the adrenalin going; makes you feel good.'

And how old are you now, do you think you will think the same when you are in your fifties, sixties, seventies? Or is aikido only for young, fit and able people?

'We don't have any old people in our dojo so that doesn't apply, it's not for wimps; it's a martial art.'

Aha, a martial art? So what was the prime ethos of the founder then?

'Who?'

The founder of aikido, the one we call O-Sensei and bow to at the beginning of every class.

'Ah, yes, move out of the way, take control and apply technique until they tap to surrender.'

So it wasn't this then?

"Aikido is not a technique to fight with or defeat the enemy. It is the way to reconcile the world and make human beings one family."

Morihei Ueshiba, Founder of Aikido.

Can't you do that without mats?

Written by some old chap who has taught weapons for over 5 years in a hall without mats.

***

54. Value of weapons by Tony Sargeant (6th dan Aikikai)

"For over 45 years I have trained with weapons as fifty percent of my practice. O-Sensei clearly trained with weapons, yet over my years of aikido training, I have had to listen to the diverse arguments over the need or not to train with them.

Now, I have reached a point in my training, where I no longer need them to aid my own practise – they have already done their job.

I realise that concentrating on body movements does not

develop the footwork as well as training with weapons. Nage often struggles to find correct footwork in taijutsu but had they taken up weapons training, their footwork would have become automatic and allowed a deeper understanding of the art to be reached.

I do not think O-Sensei used weapons just because he liked them.'

Over the years, many students have requested a Jo class, because they find the freedom of expression and variance of use with the Jo much more interesting than the ken.

I realise from this that we have let our students down by not clearly stating the purpose behind weapons training. We owe it to our teachers, masters like Saito Sensei, to honour the founder's teaching, just as he did. Saito Sensei asked us to keep the art alive and safe – and this meant the weapons legacy too.

If you really have an interest in following O-Sensei but your own style does not train in weapons, there are clips on youtube to watch and after that it is up to you to find time and space. It will be worth it.

Apart from the essential footwork emphasised and instilled by weapons, there are other gifts too.

Receiving an all out attack from a weapon allows you to come to terms with panic and fear and guide you to correct positioning with an adversary. Without pressurised training such as this you will never know if your version of the art works in the street. It may be too late by then.

The photo shows a completed move. The power, stability of hips and feet, allow mind and body to become one with the attacker. It is not **seen** but it is **felt** by both – to me this is O-Sensei's gift and why weapons should be part of your training."   *Tony Sargeant.*

***

55. Same as the Dodo - is Aikido's goose cooked?

I've been practising aikido since about 1974 and I'm only just beginning to develop a new and worthwhile understanding. I've seen people who I believe really understand the essence of aikido, though I still struggle to find the way they achieve it. I would like to share what I now know with anyone who is interested. Therein lies the problem – no one is! I teach Aiki weapons, Jo and Ken and have done as a dedicated weapons class since 2008. These isolated years of training and exploring have opened up new and rewarding insights.

It's about connection within self, about victory over self, overcoming the habits and reactions that we unerringly developed over the years to our detriment. The greatest power comes from relaxation. The lightest touch of thumb and forefinger on the Jo can overcome almost any opposing physical strength. To understand this, it is required to understand what is meant by relaxation. Videos and books can rarely if ever express the essence of the art of aikido, though they may on occasions show you a suitable gateway. Once again, a recurring theme shows itself, what you really need is not what it appears to be. In fact, what you desire you can have, by doing the opposite of what you think you need. Never add strength, if anything remove strength, to find real power. Opposites have immense power, as does relaxation.

However, the key to much success will come from your **mind** –

your greatest friend and
yet your greatest enemy.

You must learn alone but, to do so, you need the company of others.
Our modern, progressive world with all its impatient information and frenzied, tense activity finds little time for an inner journey that takes a lifetime . . . or more.
Eventually, this modern way of life could draw people into a dark age of wide spread mental illnesses . . . and there may not be a lamp left burning for them to find their way out.
Aikido has a beneficial spiritual quality, or at least it should have.
Even if O-Sensei's aikido dies out and its bones lie in the ashes with those of the Dodo, my own personal journey does not feel as though it was wasted, despite the disappointment of no new students to enjoy the same.

***

56. Can we disappear?

I've put some thought into this. . . but am minded of an old saying,

"all ye who search for certainty,
abandon hope."

In Wudang mountain a Taoist monk once said to us visiting students, "seeing is not seeing." In that fortunately receptive moment I understood what he meant. **Illusion;** almost all is illusion, all colour that we see is not real, it is an illusion created by our mind so that we can distinguish our environment. Our sight is illusion too in that the 'blind spot' that we all have in our eyes cannot be found by trying to find it in the space in front of us. The brain knows that something should be there and creates an image that fills the blind spot. The blind spot has disappeared from our vision. When you look in the mirror you rarely see yourself as you really are, you see an image that is your perception of who you think you are.

Magicians work their magic and make things disappear in front of our eyes; it is a trick, our mind sees what it thinks the eyes have seen and if the eyes have missed something, then the brain just makes something up that fits.

I read somewhere that when attacked, **O-Sensei seemed to disappear**, much to the surprise of the attacker. Note that to the observer, nothing of the sort seemed to happen, therefore we can presume that it has something to do with the impression felt by the attacker alone.

My own novice view is that this surprise was multi layered.

Let's consider the implications for our own learning if we want to emulate O-Sensei's skills. What he did, we may never know. What he might have done, we can explore.

Perhaps Uke is distracted; by a movement across his eye-line. A 'temporary blinding' either because their sight is obstructed or that their eyes followed a particular movement and took their mind with it; if their mind has gone from where nage was and followed something else ... then has nage 'disappeared'?

Eyes are an essential component of your power, your ability and your understanding. We can test this easily by pushing on someone who stands in good posture and whose eyes are looking forward, yet when they look down they are more easily moved. . . their eyes and their intention are no longer one with their body.

The next thing to consider is the simple physical level. This is where you don't visually disappear but physically to the Uke you feel like you have.

Uke directs a force towards Nage and makes contact, this satisfies Uke that his purpose is being fulfilled. . . as long as certain criteria are met by Nage that is. Retaining the point of contact Nage can withdraw his body and neutralise the force.

Neutralise is the better description than deflect or avoid

or any other word that you might substitute. Uke's body experience is that everything is alright and going to plan, Uke has put the force exactly where they wanted and it has not been interfered with, therefore they continue with what to the observer is a senseless strike. . . however, Uke's eyes tell a different tale, all has gone wrong, they have missed their target. Their target is no longer where they thought it was, it has 'disappeared'. The strange thing is

we trust our body more than our eyes

and the Uke inexplicably continues to apply force in their chosen direction; Uke cannot feel any hard resistance but is aware that there is still 'something' tangible there to push; so they do, to no avail. For Nage's part they have retained a passive presence at the point of contact while being active in moving the rest of their body, storing their own power as they do so. Nage is active in setting up their own posture and energy to advantage at the same time as Uke's attack is failing.

Where Nage places their Ki or imagination is important and you should not be surprised if it is in a direction totally against logical thought. . . for logical thought has no place in this 'magic'. Keep an open mind on this and explore it for yourself. The Chinese have that lovely saying, "don't listen to what they say, go see."

Interrupting an attacker causes an adjustment in them that takes time. A time which is a fraction longer than your own move to intercept. Once intercepted and making contact, the tactile response time is much quicker than the visual one. This results in the attacker moving first but arriving last.

For the attacker a moment of time has disappeared.

Perhaps O-Sensei had surpassed these methods and was using an 'energy' level technique. We shouldn't really call it technique either as it is closer to 'magic'. Something few understand but at which many marvel.

The placing of one's mind outside the body can create a tangible, if subtle, presence which influences something in another person. Isn't this the 'Ki' in Aikido?

O-Sensei said that he was aware that these things happened but could not explain it. It is not really something anyone can explain or intellectualise, simply something that you 'know' exists when you 'experience' it.

My own valued and respected teacher, Sensei Tony Sargeant is not only a dedicated student of O' Sensei's aikido but has studied Tai Chi, Yoga, Healing Arts and Meditation. All of these can open portals of understanding through personal experience. During training sessions, when Sensei Tony offered his arm up to uke (initiating) it was almost impossible not to reach out to grab or push it. As soon as you did, his arm seemed to disappear, leaving a hole in space into which you were drawn. As many of you will know, this is no easy task to accomplish; try it. It was many years ago when I experienced this and even to this day I cannot achieve it myself.

I am beginning to think that Ki is real, it has a tangible existence, it can be felt, experienced, sensed, it can be used to influence others. This is such a difficult subject to write about mainly because of my limited ability and knowledge. . . but it's not going to stop me trying and perhaps you will already know it better.

You need to be able to shift your consciousness around and out of your body. Koichi Tohei's exercise using the Jo is an excellent example. With a partner in Tsuki No Kamae (basic thrust stance) hold the end of their Jo with only a light grip and put your spirit into the far end of the Jo, the end that your partner is holding. The difference between spirit close to you and spirit extended away from you is great. You can test this effect for yourself - with ki and light grip you are more effective.

Practice putting your consciousness elsewhere in the body, e.g. the ball of the foot, or the palm of the hand. Control over transferring consciousness is used in pain relief. You twist a toe on the mat. . . you can keep your mind on the toe and all its pain or shift your consciousness to e.g. palm of the hand or to your hara or centre. Not always easy, so you need practice. Meditation can assist you in such control. The pain disappears ! It is as if it were not there. Herein lays the clue to what we need to do in order to disappear.
I just hope you can find a way through these ramblings to an understanding which will be of value to you.

Try and think this way. . . there is no such thing as imagination. . . everything is real.

Whatever you 'imagine' exists, does exist.

To feel the subtlety of Ki try this exercise. Ask a partner to place their hand on your arm near the shoulder. They should push only lightly but steady.
Stand relaxed but with life. Put your consciousness in your head behind the third eye, sense that this place opens and becomes alive. Move to the heart area and do the same thing with your consciousness, keep both centres open and alive. Now move to the Hara or centre, bring that consciousness here too, open and alive, keeping all three points open and alive. . . . it is all you think about . . no wondering, no doubt just stick to what you have been asked to do. Your partner who is applying the gentle push should feel like you at first 'disappeared' or at least became softer, and then they should feel like their whole body is gently and subtly being moved away from you.

When you are one with the universe,
the universe will help you.

In the ken partner practice of Ki Musubi No Tachi, as the attacker lifts to strike for the second time there is a point during which they are unsighted from your ken. You then enter in migi hamni with Tsuki to their chest. If you have the timing correct it is they who expose your ken to their awareness as they lift their own ken. It suddenly appears, giving them a surprise which you can see reflected in their startled body language; my point is that there are things that appear and disappear and it is this phenomena we could use to advantage. . . if we have the skill. The mind is nearly everything in this matter; that and the perfect timing born of good training.

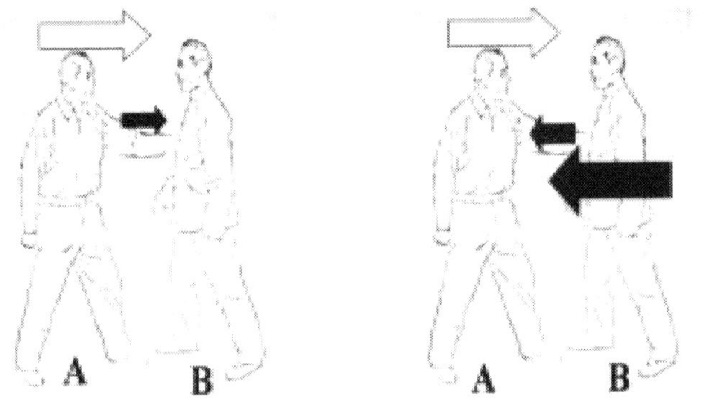

If 'A' walks towards 'B' with energy and intention to push and then withdraws the physical push at the last moment, before contact, 'B' usually senses the energy and leans in to counter it. Of course it isn't there, only the belief exists that it is. Is that not disappearing too?

Without exploration, much remains undiscovered

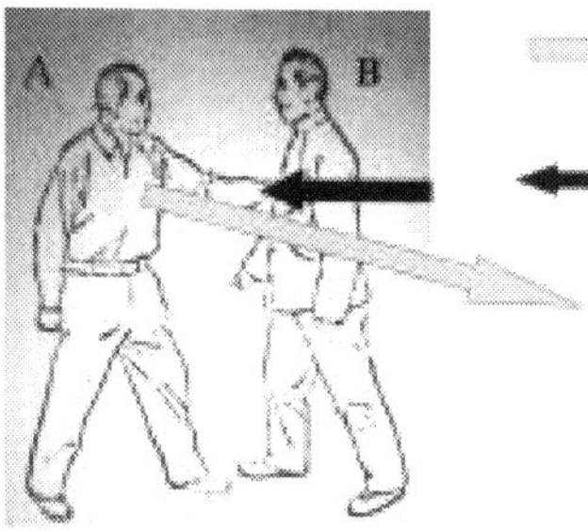

A's intent, energy and movement

B's intent energy

In this first case we have yang against yang, strength against strength and the strongest wins.
However, the following ideas do not rely upon strength.

Second case, A's intent is to push B to the star point. If B then puts his consciousness and intent to the same place, A should feel B soften and what A thought he was pushing disappears

Third case. A pushes as before but B places his consciousness in his centre. (Hara, DanTien, centre. Again A senses that what he thought he was pushing has changed, it no longer seems to be there in the form it was at the start.
'Something' has disappeared

A pushes B and B 'accepts' the energy, absorbing it until it is all neutralised. B may not have disappeared but may seem to be immovable.
A has little left to push with and senses this loss.

All of these ideas, which you can try for yourself, involve the mind... Your mind. By shifting your consciousness to a place outside your body 'something' of you will have disappeared as far as the consciousness of the person pushing goes.

57. What is your opinion on cross training within and without the art of Aikido ?

Of course we cannot ask everyone, as half the aikido teachers have made a choice already and won't be reading this, and in all likelihood nor will many of the students of those that do. That does have a convenience to it for some I am sure.
Did you train with other styles of aikido, or even with different teachers of the same style?
Did you train in other arts which taught you something of benefit to your own study of aikido? This could be a positive benefit in understanding or negative in that you realised this other art added nothing to your own learning. (Most unlikely.)
If you never tried other styles or arts are you sure that your aikido is the best it can be?
Are you confident that what you do cannot be bettered from a source other than your own teacher and style?
Have you ever wondered why some schools will never respond to you, let alone train with you? (Perhaps they are very happy and successful in their own cult like bubble, so why should anyone else mind.)
Are you convinced that only your way is true to O-Sensei? Did he actually ask you to copy him or did he ask you to embrace the principles and develop the art?

Develop it. . . not ruin it!

Do you encourage your students to attend courses and workshops by other teachers?
If not, why not? (It is usually a given that lower grades benefit from a grounding in one style before looking at another so as not to confuse. There are plenty of high grades out there who are confused too.)
If you are a student, why don't you attend workshops and seminars by other teachers?

Are you afraid you won't learn anything?
Are you afraid you will?

Wasn't aikido about reconciling the world in peace? You won't find that by building walls, will you?
I do believe that the great masters of the art of aikido had more than a brief dabble in other arts, arts which taught them something very few will find in aikido alone. Unless you think aikido is something that I don't. My own teacher and his before him, always encouraged us to go and see others and to take away that which was helpful, discarding that which was not. Such teachers are not afraid.

Are you annoyed by these questions because your stuff works okay in your dojo or in your mind?

Aikido is difficult enough, regardless of style, but to isolate ourselves from new learning is surely folly. If we think only our system, art or style is correct then we close our eyes to the gems of wisdom that may well exist in other styles (or even clubs of the same style). Who knows what another teacher, or student for that matter, has discovered that will raise your own game? And you'll never know either, unless you go see!
Isolationism may lead to extinction. Mind and body are bounded by limits ... we mainly only function within these limits. Various arts may accentuate certain qualities and they in themselves may be difficult to grasp as they are counter intuitive. Get out there, learn what is available and see how it might inform your own path in life.
Small nuances gleaned from other body arts can open doors to new understanding and also open the door to let you out of the prison you made for yourself.
I still don't know the answers. I am still often confused. I am still searching. I am going to see.

***

58. Exploring the point of contact.

I'm sure that many of you will already know a great deal more about the point of contact principles. Let us travel together a while and see where we might agree and help each other. Surely principles in aikido unite us, even if some principals may not. It's a paradox that followers of aikido sometimes fail to engage in its philosophy with other clubs, teachers or styles. This is a route to conflict and disharmony – how strange is that?

I've picked a Jo nage technique just to illustrate my current understanding about the point of contact. We all know that written articles cannot transmit perfect understanding; there's no surprise that this one's no different.

The photo shows the technique half way through and about the place where movement can often become difficult for nage, a place where they may be tempted to add force to the point of contact and so become the attacker.

If nage feels the struggle at this point
then they must be in conflict and therefore not Aiki.

They are in conflict with their partner, in conflict in their own mind and in conflict within their own body. Ego, the need to be the winner, the greater enemy living within, can prevent effective aiki. Human beings usually enjoy the feel of their own power, that desire can cause problems. (It begins the moment a baby first presses their feet against the floor – they just love that feeling). At any time you feel your own power realise that you only feel it because it is coming back to you. If it's coming back to you it is available for your opponent to use against you. At the point where you no longer feel your own physical power returning, (note carefully that this does not mean collapsing, retreating or giving in – in fact the opposite will become true) the energy of the attacker is absorbed, dissipated and confused for they no longer know where to apply their own force. (Yes, that's right, the force they thought they knew has disappeared !)

We can retain the point of contact for sensitivity
but we should not act directly upon it.

Breathing and maintaining centre is protective in itself, no extra power should be added to the point of contact as that can be self defeating. If you conflict at the point of contact the opponent will know your intention and power, in reality they are just as capable of using that information as you are.
In general, mindfully acting on the point of contact only results in conflict and struggle, often this means that the strongest will win. Also if you disturb the attacker in their chosen action then they will change how and what they do. e.g. a blocked hand might invite an elbow strike instead. (This

'non compliance' would rarely be countenanced in an aikido class, which is a shame as it relates to an important principle). Let them go where they think they want to go, let them think they are successful – in fact let them **feel** that they have succeeded. Though their eyes will clearly tell them that they have failed, their body tells them otherwise. The mind will almost inevitably believe body over sight and the attacker will ignore the truth told by their eyes.

Back to our specific Jo nage example; a sincere, uncompromising and mindful use of, in this case, the right hip results in a harmony at the point of contact with the attacker. It also allows retention of a balanced centre throughout. Everything moves around that centre and remains the case whether using the hips or stepping.

There should be no slack in the body, or mind either, as you should be as one, united in principles; a relaxed concentration with open joints should permeate your entire body, in relaxation, energy can flow.

Major blocking points for our own energy are shoulders, neck and hips;

The block is caused by tension. For all the skills of many Aikidoka, their own understanding of body awareness is often sparse or non existent. I believe this to be an error in many of our studies and may well find correction in Ki style exercises and some mind/body meditations too.

Avoid putting your own mind at the point of contact; and deprive them of any messages of conscious intent.

If the opponent is unaware of the intention or location of your power then they will find it difficult to respond.

Remember, they will believe their body over their eyes.

To enable whole body power at the physical level, and this is where body awareness comes in, you need to cross connect your body, i.e. opposite arms and hips. This cross connection of the body creates great internal power – why would you not want it? There is nothing wrong with being powerful, just take care how you use it.
How often has the teacher said, "use your hips"?

> ***But how often has the teacher said,***
> ***"this is how to use your hips."?***

How, is very important and training with weapons is a useful mechanism to exploit the understanding we need.
It's too much to go into here but the hip should feel like it is melting away, disappearing, it is not a solid feeling of engagement. It's all about body awareness and the intelligent use of mind.
Power can be delivered to the point of contact or more accurately power travels through the point of contact without force, without conflict. Providing you do not act mindfully at that point itself.

***

"The simplest of technique contains
the most profound principles."

***

59. Peace or Conflict? A choice?

O-Sensei wanted aikido to reconcile the world in peace.
A noble and worthy sentiment, but is it possible?
Without conflict where does your aikido get you?

Why did he do this?

How did he do that?

For anything to exist there must be an opposite. What you read now is dark and you are only aware of it because the background is light, if the background was dark the words would disappear . . . you need opposites for existence. You may find opposites written here, you may disagree with what is written, this too is valid.
To make progress, doing technique, forms or methods is not enough, there is something else, in fact, it is that which would appear to be the exact opposite of what you think you are studying.

"You cannot make butter by churning sand."

Let's explore just one idea for personal development in Aiki, that of opposition. The Chinese use the expressions Yin and Yang, (Yin is passive, Yang is active. From 'Aikido and the Harmony of Nature' by Mitsugi Saotome. "*In Kannagara the counterparts of Yin and Yang are* aramitma, *spirit of firmness and strength, and* nigimitama, *spirit of flexibility and gentleness*."
They are opposites but not necessarily in conflict, they complement each other in harmony. Is this not Aiki? That for which you seek?
Is it possible that at the centre between the opposing forces there is a 'magical' place where you can engage with the inner, innate you, and be in tune with the universal Ki.
We'll try and look at some practical matters but I hope you will be able to look further at how your very soul, your way of living might change too.
I'm going to presume that you have some aikido basics, in particular with the Jo. Let's use the basic thrust or Tsuki for our purpose.
Pick up your Jo or even pretend you have one, make a thrust and stay there for a while as you consider how it 'feels', your posture, your balance, your power.
In the process of making Tsuki there are many subtle movements, too many to consider here, except for the basic

large physical movement forward. Remember that we said earlier that we must have an opposite? We obviously cannot match the physical forward thrust with a physical backwards one, for both of these are Yang or active. What we can use though is Yin, physically moving, no, but energetically moving, yes. Your mind, Ki, Chi, Yi, imagination, pretence, call it what you will, can project back on the same plane as the forward thrust. Your energy flows in both directions but the emphasis is backwards. . . almost like it is the propulsive force that drives the Jo physically forward.
Try your basic thrust again then project your mind back along the line that the Jo took. Stay a while and 'feel' what has happened. You should find that you are more stable, centred, and relaxed, you will be more powerful and in more than one direction. . . get someone to test you.

The place you have found is that 'magic' place where the inner you resides and is at peace.

Relaxation leads to opening of the body and opening the body leads to space, the space in which the real power seems to live, the essence itself.
Ai ki do . . harmony spirit way . . . note it doesn't mention body.
Opening up the body with the mind to find the 'space' has some odd side effects, for example, it may expose old injuries that you have been shielding with tight muscle and, odd as it may seem, it can release emotional memories that were locked in the body too. (Leading to strange dreams, flashbacks and the like.)
These are the 'layers' we added to our innate self as we went through life.
Practising other arts like yoga or tai chi can help to open the body and by continuing to practice through these layers you can come out the other side and be closer to who you always really were.

The journey is the goal and is ever onward; the innate in you was always there – can you find it again? To quote an old Chinese saying,

"Peace lies not in the world,
but in the man who walks the path."

So, the question was, 'peace or conflict', I think if you can access the space ***between,*** then you can touch both and there find a harmony you otherwise would never realise existed. . . an enlightenment of sorts.

***

"Ego is a false God
that too many people love to worship,
often without knowing it."

***

60. On the benefits of workshops and courses.

"This day is called the feast of Crispian: He that outlives this day, and comes safe home, will stand a tip-toe when the day is named, And rouse him at the name of Crispian. He that shall live this day, and see old age, Will yearly on the vigil feast his neighbours, And say 'To-morrow is Saint Crispian:' Then will he strip his sleeve and show his scars. And say 'These wounds I had on Crispin's day.' " *History of Henry V*

Okay, so it's a bit over the top but the sentiments remain true. What can we **gain** from a workshop or seminar that goes beyond our normal class? What can we **give** too? There are many gifts; the greatest is to yourself, then there is the support you give to the local teacher and the guest teacher, a support

without which clubs would eventually fall into oblivion. . . so your gift includes the perpetuation of the art. There is the gift of your own knowledge, given without ego; the gift of friendship between strangers; the gift of joy in sharing O-Sensei's art; the gift of question to the teacher who will learn from your question alone, whatever your level.
So what do we get out of it?

Mainly we get as much as we are prepared to give, it is mutual.

Without a training partner your quest is fruitless; as is a teacher without a student.
What keeps us from attending workshops? Perhaps you have sound reasons why attendance is not possible and after all it is your life in which you must do your best for all. Perhaps you have darker reasons for not attending and they relate to your own problems and insecurities. Perhaps you should question the depth to which you follow O-Sensei's ethics. I do. If you are annoyed by this then you probably don't!
I attended the 25th May Bukiwaza workshop hosted by Mark Allcock of Wellsprings Aikido in Dorset, taught by Sensei McGlone of TIA Europe; the subject was 13 Jo Kata and associated awase. I was also honoured to be asked to teach at the Wellsprings Club Friday night class the night before the workshop. Teaching is one of the greatest tools to learning. . . you soon find out if you are in error. There were things I could show and those I could not, some of which I'd thought were fairly problem free. We specifically looked at the strengths and weaknesses of pins. . . but how wrong can you be when a 4th kyu so easily evades your pin. When I was younger and stronger I would have used just that to try and win but now I know I must find a path that is successful by other means.

We need errors and failures; it is what shows us the truth of the matter and it is at the heart of our learning.

If we don't embrace challenge and step out of our comfort zone how can we ever progress, except perhaps in our imagination.

Later that evening I had a conversation with Sensei Mark about the subject of reality in aikido and what constituted reality. It moved on to practical evasion from kihon; He gripped my wrist and I thought, 'I know too much, I will move easily and he will be surprised'; the surprise was all mine as I couldn't move. He explained that he was 'cheating' as he called it by making small changes to posture that countered my moving. Is that cheating? Is it not also a reality?

I already have much to think about and we haven't even started the Bukiwaza workshop yet.

The day of the 13 Jo kata workshop. When we arrived at the venue, a really beautiful village sports facility bathed in sunshine, some students were already there and everyone happily helped to carry in what was needed; another gift, the joy of willing people sharing a task. Some students came late, an hour late. All the way from Reading, the Bank holiday traffic had taken its toll on their travels; another gift arrives, understanding, empathy, sympathy, welcoming smiles.

When asked by Sensei, all present accepted that they already knew the 13 count Jo Kata, and we did too. . . our version of it anyway. We were asked to demonstrate as Sensei counted the moves. We received our first big correction after the very first move. Any guesses? You'll have done it at some time and almost certainly will again! Don't look down. . . your feet have been with you a long time, you shouldn't need to look when you place the tip of the Jo on the ground. Of course, silly us, we knew that didn't we? How annoying that we let ourselves down before we even started. We often 'know' something that we would correct in others and yet we fall into the same trap. . . this in itself is a giant learning point.

Other corrections followed, accompanied by sound reasoning why it should be so. There are other ways, but the logic of the method shown was indisputable, so lots of room for thought again. There was much emphasis on blending. . . . ah yes we know that too . . . but this was deeper than we had thought to go. It was about connecting, sensing breath, energy and intention in your partner so that you effect a true harmony and not just blend to escape. If anything it was blend to become one. Most notably in the 2nd move of the kata awase, using their energy to drive the movement of high speed turn and strike. No wasted foot movements that rob you of time, everything efficiently executed. 3rd tsuki from your partner is not blocked and almost not parried either, just softly blended and deflected. I'd been working for several months on a powerful counter deflection prior to completing the tsuki but Sensei McGlone's version didn't do this, it merely changed direction and was easily lined up for the finishing tsuki. There were many such events, all of which were ably demonstrated with accompanying explanation; though it was not needed as the effectiveness of the demonstration was evident. Key points? True blending at a deeper level, awareness, no wasted movements, know when and how to move off line as necessary, blend with the partner's energy. . . engage with it and use it to power your own sense of movement.

For me it was a wonderful weekend with the blessings of fine weather, good food, great friends and good teaching. . . it enabled me the privilege of several more steps on the spiritual pathway.

What can you get from attending a workshop?
Everything, absolutely everything,
just keep an open mind about you.

You simply cannot beat, being there!

"Physical technique has a limit."

***

61. When does it change from mind to body?

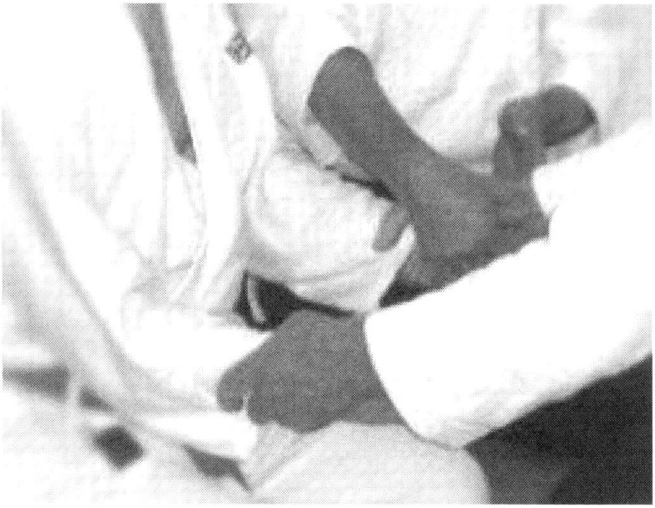

A good practitioner 'feels' the technique

'Excuse me sensei, do you put the foot here or here?'
Not an uncommon question in an aikido class as the student seeks to affect the uke like the teacher did. Sometimes the answer is obviously simple, verbal and comes from basics and the mind. Sometimes however, the teacher is not sure of how to answer. What do they do? They perform the technique again but this time they observe where they put their own foot, and say, 'place your foot here, just so.'
This teacher had developed body conscious skills which told him when the move was correct, it was a level beyond thinking. therefore any art which develops body consciousness can assist the aikido practitioner to 'find' the right place through that knowing. If you only learn it technically by mind memory you may find it harder to adapt to the changes required in more advanced partner practise.
Listen to your body, it knows what is a correct posture .... without your brain's input !

62. Consider the 'mind' of the jo !

Recently I've been working on the harmony between the travel of weapon and self. (Helped by entertaining the thought that the weapon will always prefer to travel in line with the grain of the wood.)

A weapon in motion along a path that has no conflict with universal principles will feel in total harmony with your body .... which is also adhering to the same principles. This is difficult to achieve if you grip too tightly as your joints are not free to sense the correct path. We also covered the act of gripping earlier in the book, by reason of its importance.

"The correct path already exists -
all you need do is allow your body to find it."

Even greater harmony exists if your grip concentrates on the little finger and its neighbour. All movement is free and relaxed, smooth yet still powerful and unifies the mind, body and weapon.

Using first finger prioritised gripping tightens the body and prevents you 'feeling' the correct path.

Why not experiment with the idea?

I do not doubt what my experience tells me is either correct or better than what I did before.

63. Do martial arts rely on not being the attacker?

(A small truth about mind and body relating to martial arts.)

This is a question relating to traditional martial arts and not necessarily to sports or self defence arts. I know a bit about Aikido and some tai chi but you must be the judge of this article's relevance to your own art.

Our mind is our most powerful friend and our worst enemy. Our body will listen to our mind and, with the right mind/body engagement, perform amazing feats with effortless power. (Because it commands muscle use beyond the simple and beyond our physical awareness of their engagement.)

Our eyes too are a powerful tool, not just for observing what is going on, but for a much deeper purpose, they have an ability to connect our spirit to the outside world. Blocking a punch with eyes open is powerful but the identical punch blocked when blinking is much weaker. Regardless of how hard you might try.

So, we know that the body is capable of effortless and seemingly limitless power. (Look at free climbers on great cliffs or mountains.) We know that the mind can control this power and that our eyes contribute to physical power.

However, our mind will believe what the body tells it over what the eyes do. For example, a very gently deflected punch will leave the attacker with a good feeling – one of success – but they have failed – the eyes tell them clearly that they have missed the target but the mind prioritises the body's verdict. This can be a useful skill for the defender but not easy to learn.

The body can also be fooled by a soft touch into believing that all is safe even if the mind and eyes are fully aware that a hard strike is to follow. The following attack has far greater impact because the body itself is unprepared.

In my opinion this is a valuable principle to follow (in Aikido) and why we should not become the attacker. Not because it is

some evil act but because this way the attacker's mind is fooled into their own defeat.
It is all about what happens at the point of contact – or more importantly doesn't happen!
Signals are received quicker by touch than by sight, so avoid giving physical or mental information by touch but instead try and receive them. Thoughts moving to action and eye to brain signals all take time, if you can interfere with the attacker's process, they must reset their decision clock back to zero, allowing you to complete your move faster than them.

Do not all styles claim to follow the principle of not becoming the attacker?
However, we rarely realise fully what this means. If we use direct force against our attacker then we are breaking the principle. At higher levels it can be seen that even the mere act of intention itself is enough to become the attacker. An act of intention alone is transmitted to aware others and therefore is of use to them in defeating us.
It's fairly obvious that much of this is counter intuitive to human beings in normal life and definitely not easy to attain, let alone master.

Just something to consider in traditional martial arts.

I'm sorry if I have not made some things clear enough but perhaps you will discover the truth of the matter as you explore your own journey.

Section 3 Amusement Only

64 . Insights for new students in Aikido.

If you are coming on our mat,
make sure that you are, not too fat,
and if you really want to win,
make sure that you are, not too thin.

If you want to learn to save,
when joining us, you need be brave.
But also useful, so I hear,
is, never lose, your sense of fear.

Always heed, the teacher wise,
then question what he does advise.
Practise well and peace you'll gain,
as long as you don't mind the pain.

Keen students fine, come through the door,
they love it all, they love the floor.
Once gi is bought with stroke of pen,
we won't be seeing them again.

On my advice, don't come to blows,
Aikido's secrets – no one knows.
Strength of gnat or strength of ox,
all Aikido - paradox.

***

65. The new uchideshi.

Extracts of an imagined conversation at an aikido seminar, begins with a self centred student . . .

"So, a little bird tells me you have an uchideshi *[live in student}* now. . . things must be looking up at your club these days."
"Yes, we're very lucky; she has all the attributes of a master, even at her young years."
"Oh, so it's a she. What's she look like then?"
"Short, well built, fair hair, brown eyes, quite attractive actually and has a friendly tactile personality, I like her a lot."
"So, what's the missus think about that then, bit jealous eh?"
"No, my wife is very understanding and in fact gets on very well with Elsa. OK they might have fell out a couple of times but all in all we are quite happy the three of us. In fact you could learn a lot yourself from Elsa. . . change your lifestyle it would. . . and your aikido would improve too."
"Oh yeah, of course it would. So just what's so good about this smarty pants Elsa uchideshi then that she could improve my lifestyle."
"Ok. if you really want to know; she eats a proper balanced diet that suits her body type. . . and sticks to it too ... no cheating ever. Keeps clean, likes swimming, and washes frequently. She rests at the right times. . . she realises when the body needs to regenerate and sleeps. . . no forcing herself to stay up and watch TV or check the computer for messages. In training she is energy sensitive, loyal, trustworthy, totally attentive, moves well, using the whole body in a relaxed but powerful and totally coordinated way and uses the eyes in a focussed manner. . . much like the eyes of a predator, taking everything in, missing nothing. Despite being self driven and determined she listens and follows instructions willingly, not once has she questioned my teaching, not once has she criticised me behind my back. She is an excellent student. I think she is in it for life and not for the occasional socialising like so many students can be these days.

We haven't had to spend a lot of money on bedding etc as she seems happy to sleep on the floor. . . it must be good for her back or something. We have of course supplied blankets and crockery and she has the run of half the house. I strongly suspect she is highly intelligent but has never spoken to us yet about her ideas. . . . She is just totally natural with a good personality and gets on with everyone she meets".

"Sounds a right creep if you ask me. . . anyway I'm off for a beer and a pizza now . . . I'll let you know sometime if I am coming to one of your workshops. I'd like to meet this Elsa, perhaps she'd like to come out for a drink with me. Gotta go, see ya ...."

Another student arrived, "Hi sensei, was that one of your old training partners you were just chatting with?"
"Yes, I was telling him about Elsa, our new live in student."
"I thought Elsa was your Labrador dog; did he realise you were talking about a dog?"
"You are right and no he didn't. . . but I think secretly he was so impressed by the description I gave him that he's now looking forward to taking her out! Strange thing is, she won't judge him and will probably go".

Their minds wandered briefly to the day dream world; they smiled and they laughed.

Happy days, Elsa uchideshi days.

66. Dojo, is it a place, or an instruction . . . ?

67. A tale of two Gi's

I hope you might find this a humorous tale about Gi's .... Unless of course you have one the same! *(Gi; a term I am using to describe the heavy duty white pyjama like clothing as used in Judo, Karate and Aikido).*

So often they seem ill fitting, and on occasions you might just wonder what sort of animal they were made for ..... Certainly not human at times I suspect.. perhaps made to fit O-Uke, the Yeti like brute you always fear will one day attend the seminar for which you have just booked, despite still sporting a slowly recovering injury.
It reminds me of many years ago when I had a peasant like job for the Government's civil engineering laboratories. Apart from a pair of rubber boots, a pencil, ruler, chair, desk and name on the shared office door, they issued me with a pair of

overalls; a sort of boiler suit affair. They looked good until I tried them on and found they did not fit .... anywhere! Walking in them was difficult as the crotch of the garment was closer to my knees than my groin. 'No problem', I thought, 'just take them back to stores.'
I found the store-man and explained, "I'm sorry but these overalls don't fit me."
The simple apology and exchange I expected did not come to pass, the store-man simply looked up over his glasses and said, "I'm sorry too, but if a Ministry boiler suit fits you then you're deformed."

I've often wondered if the same applies to the Gi.
(Apologies to any finely built folk out there that actually have perfectly fitting Gi.)
Somewhere in the world in a Gi factory, far, far away, the quality control manager ... on a bag of nuts a day and only part time ... is looking at a collection of misshapen but otherwise well made garments. "Mmm," he thinks, "somehow we need to get rid of this lot." He calls over an old chap, probably a foreign cousin of the Ministry store-man. "Sort these into pairs, that is a top and a bottom together and put them in plastic bags .... There's a selection of labels over there, just find one that seems about right and stick it on. I'll go and arrange shipping to the UK; they're usually a good bet for this stuff."
A few months later in the UK, an Aikidoka takes possession of his new Gi, confident in its quality as it was recommended by his teacher who said he made no profit from the sale and that he knew lots of people who wore theirs with pride and satisfaction ... mainly at other clubs apparently.
"Right, here we go," said the Aikidoka to himself standing in his Woolworth's underpants, "let's try the trousers first."
He tried to pull them up to his waist, but something was stopping them being pulled right up, ... yes ... it was his groin! Staring down in disbelief he could see that between crotch and

waist band there was only a hand's width of material. "Mmm," he pondered, as he strained to pull the cord through the waist band that was too narrow for the amount of cord, finally he manages to make a bow knot that has a remote but hopeful chance of keeping these 'hipster' style Gi trousers from slipping down, "Not to worry, the Gi top will bridge the gap."

Looking down at the crisp starch white Gi trousers he observes the knee pad patches and decides to try them out. Our Aikidoka kneels in seiza, the back of the trousers slip lower still and expose what is commonly termed 'builder's bum', and there in full view, resting nowhere near under his knees but on his upper legs are a pair of crisp starch white reinforced knee pads.

He stands and looking in the mirror consoles himself, "Oh, well, not to worry, at least the leg length is good if I fold them up a turn or two."

He consoles self yet again, "They're not too bad for thirty quid, and they do have some lovely embroidered oriental writing on the label." ….. Little does he realise that these are merely essential laundry instructions that he can never knowingly follow and not the warrior like spiritual aphorisms that he thinks they are. Then there was the classic half hippo half kangaroo animal he saw as a beautifully embroidered dragon.

Picking up the plastic bag he tips out the Gi top. He looks briefly at the bag before placing it on the nearby bench. It read, 'dagner extinguish life, not wearbag,'

"Crumbs," he thought, "they could do with an interpreter never mind a tailor".

The Gi jacket slipped on easily, the arms were a good length … conveniently about the same length as his own … the body of the jacket is comfortingly long and overlaps his low slung waist band easily. He suddenly feels good and acts out an imaginary technique in front of the all admiring mirror. He contemplates how swish he will look on the tatami in his new Gi … 'ah, the envy of all who watch' …. he thought.

"Enough of this, young man", he says to himself, "Let's try the belt on..... See if we remember how to tie it eh?" He crossed the jacket left over right - "er, or was that right over left," he thought.
He busied himself watching his hands wrap the belt around his body twice and then make several attempts to have a flat knot that pointed in the right direction. At last it was done, mind you there seemed to be almost enough spare belt left over for another trip around his midriff. Still, perhaps he would grow into it, you know, develop a good centre as they say.
Dressing now complete he eagerly anticipated admiring his latest martial attire in the mirror, oh, how good he felt, how magnificent he would be at class, he could hardly wait.
Then horror of all horrors, the image that looked back at him from the mirror was not remotely how he had seen it in his mind. The Jacket was fine at the bottom but at the top it didn't meet at all, leaving half an acre of hairy chest exposed. Even tugging it from both sides did not help ... it was just simply short of material.
Even at his level he could envisage a new and unexpected life experience on the mat, as while his scrunched waist band cut mercilessly into his hips and with his Sensei's voice ringing in his ears, "get those trousers shortened before you lose a toe in them," some gorilla like uke would be tearing out handfuls of chest hair instead of gripping his gaping lapels.
Oh well, not to worry, at least it was a lot better than his previous Gi.

68. Not just Gi's apparently !

I read the Gi tale, had a really good laugh, you have to have trained in martial arts to really appreciate how true it is. It reminded me when I once bought a 'box' through my club sensei, 'these are the ones to wear' he told me, 'great protection'. I was not sure, everybody had cloth pouches and this one was mesh, he assured me it was the one for me.(even though he did not wear this sort himself). Oh well I thought, it must be ok. I wore it twice before all the mesh started to tear and fall to pieces. This is not right, I thought, as everyone else was saying they bought theirs from a magazine for half the price, and they were cloth, in fact everyone's was cloth. So I took it back to my sensei and showed him the problem! 'What have you been doing with this?' he said. 'Just wearing it', I answered. 'You must sweat a lot', he said. (I thought everyone did). Perhaps you can sew it together,' then I complained about it being uncomfortable. He looked confused, so I said, 'don't worry.''No,' he said 'I will send it back to suppliers and see what they say!'

I never heard any more and bought one from a magazine like everyone else. I wonder where it is now and whose groin it's protecting, or did someone have it before me? Support your club!!!! *Anonymous*

***

69. Dojo training excuses;

Can't come tonight I have some new shoes.
If it was in winter, I'd come.
If it was in summer, I'd come.
It's too late.
It's too early.
It's too hot.
It's too cold.
I can't lift my arms up like this so I can't do that.
My husband says it's rubbish, he used to do Judo you know.
I've just had my dinner.
I need to eat.
Must pack as I'm on holiday next week.

Excuses not given ... they usually select one from above instead of any of these;
Football on telly tonight,
I haven't washed my feet.
My gi is still in the wash from last week.
I did a nasty technique on that big bloke last week and I'm waiting for him to forget - or take up another art.

***

70. The Yonkyo class;

It was a week long, live in, training session at the Dojo, I was there training when I could (or felt like it!) and happened to ask why we hadn't trained in yonkyo for some time. As you mostly know it's an often excruciatingly painful pressure point technique on the thumb side inner wrist .... a bit like elbowing something hard with your funny bone, that sort of feeling. (I was told once by a Belgian instructor that constant pressure on this point can cause unconsciousness ... not sure if it is true but no one I know would want to explore the idea any further.) Well the teacher agreed that it was worth revisiting and planned it for the first class in the afternoon.
Over lunch I had a chance to look around the garden and saw lots of jobs that really needed doing ... urgently too as I thought at the time ... so I made my excuses for missing the class. They still did yonko ... for about an hour and a half .... as you know it is bad etiquette to scream out loud in the dojo ... unless it is a kiai of course. As I worked away on pruning and edging lawns around the building I could hear their silent screams passing through the walls and into outer space.

They seemed to enjoy it and all thanked me warmly of course at tea break.

71. Keeping the way.

We all, that walk this path shall find,
sharp thorns, that seek to tear and bind.
When darkness falls, the way seems long,
but trouble not, our minds are strong.
With hearts of oak and faith that's blind
we'll find at last, this path is kind.

**

We all sit around in a ring and suppose,
but the secret sits in the middle and knows.'

Robert Frost

At the time of writing, the author teaches a weekly weapons class in North Devon.

Any student of any level will always find a welcome there.

Consistent and correct practise will create the mind-body pathways that allow an almost spiritual natural power to be produced .... there is only one path to this place !

Thank you for reading this book.

Be not afraid of going slowly –
only of being still.

Only by being one with that of the
universe, that which willingly carries you
safely through life, will you fulfil your true
destiny – whatever that is.

Printed in Poland
by Amazon Fulfillment
Poland Sp. z o.o., Wrocław

56185765R00132